A Note to the Reader

Some of the "postcards" in this book relate travel experiences that are more than a decade old. Over the years, changes may have occurred resulting in, for example, a new name for an airport, a different owner for a railway or rearrangement of a museum wing. Markets have issued new currencies, such as the euro. For the sake of clarity and authenticity, I've preserved the facts as each traveler experienced them.

Also by Gina Greenlee

THE CHEAPER THAN THERAPY SERIES

How to Keep Life's Small Problems from Becoming Big ones
The Lesson of the Paper Clips

How to Take Risks to Create the Life You Want
The Lesson of the Chopsticks

Cover and interior design by
Dana Robinson

Postcards

&

PEARLS™

*Life Lessons
from Solo Moments
on the Road*

Gina Greenlee

First Edition

Aventine Press
1023 4th Avenue, Suite 204
San Diego, CA 92101
ISBN: 1-59330-537-0
Library of Congress Control Number: 2008926407
Library of Congress Cataloging-in-Publication Data

Printed in the United States of America

In memory of

Joan Lee

Introduction

The first time I traveled solo I was 16 years old. It was only to the movie theater but I was at an age when who you hang with – or don't – defines you in the eyes of the crowd. I wanted to see the movie *Orca*. My friends didn't. I agonized over missing the film. After a few hours I thought, *To heck with it; I'm going alone.*

I chewed my nails during the entire bus ride to the theater, worried that the ticket clerk might pity me when I said, "One, please," or that groups of movie-goers would assume I had no friends. The truth is no one gave me a second look. The world thinking I was a loser for going to the movies by myself existed only in my mind.

The lights dimmed and the projector rolled. Afterward, as moviegoers streamed out of one showing and filed in for the next, I nestled into my seat and thought, *I can sit here all day if I want to.*

I gleefully watched *Orca* twice.

Until that rainy Sunday at the movies 31 years ago, for me, companionship had been a mandate for life's good times. After *Orca*, it became a choice. My trip to the theater helped me to distinguish between loneliness (experienced by default), and solitude (choosing when and how to enjoy my own company), as I began a journey of engaging the world on my own terms. Over the years, that journey deepened as I traveled life's roads with increasing independence and confidence, whether I was attending graduate school at night while working during the day, buying my first house or changing careers.

Postcards and Pearls: Life Lessons from Solo Moments on the Road celebrates this journey of joy, discovery and personal evolution. Through 118 "postcards," I, along with 17 other women, share stories of traveling on our own. By depending on ourselves – whether we encountered new pleasures, navigated old fears or teetered on the edges of comfort – each experience taught us transformative lessons or "pearls" of wisdom that we carried back home.

In these pages, traveling "solo" does not necessarily mean "alone." The absence of other people often suggests regretful isolation. "Solo" by contrast, is a willful decision to be the architect of our own experience. On the road, that might mean being completely on our own, hiring a guide, joining a group of people we've never met before, or carving out solo time while traveling with family or friends. Off the road, it could mean visiting a museum or attending a play or workshop in our own company.

In *Postcards and Pearls*, you'll meet Kerry, a college professor who writes, "I spent most of one summer involved in other people's activities. But when I traveled with my parents and one of my sisters to Martha's Vineyard for a week, I finally figured out a way to be alone.

"At the end of one of the main streets in Vineyard Haven is a massage center. This street is usually crowded with tourists shopping for jewelry, books or Vineyard artwork. The sidewalk ends at the massage center, causing most tourists to turn around. I took this as an invitation – no, as confirmation – that things could only get better. Inside the center, the cool conditioned air was enough to make me pay the owner. They scheduled me for the next day, just after lunch. It was great to say to my parents and my sister, 'I have plans. See you all later.' Surprise, they had plans, too. I was delighted that they didn't care…"

You'll also hear from Marita: "I am not a solitary person. As the mother of four children [and] wife of 37 years, there have been few times in my life when I have done anything alone. And, for the most part, I have loved it that way." But later in life, Marita's job as a university department head required that she travel solo regularly during her marriage. Then, she became a widow. "How fortunate I am that I began to take these steps before my husband died," Marita continues. "I doubt I would have been able to begin this new way of being and doing after the devastation of such a loss."

And Jan, an author and researcher, writes about her solo weekend while married with children: "I was a 40-something wife and mother, working and going to school part time. And, I was weary. I needed to get away and, for the first time, I did not consider asking a relative or friend to come with me… traveling solo was the beginning of an amazing off-road journey. I became less fearful, willing to take more risks, which soon gave me the confidence to take on new and bigger challenges. When a business acquaintance asked me to help with seminars that her company was conducting, I was able to put aside my fear of public speaking, which eventually led to an exciting new career."

The gift of solo moments is that they are wholly ours. On or off the road, solo moments connect us inward to ourselves with heightened clarity and insight. They also direct our energies out into the world, magnetizing us to new people and experiences we may not have encountered under any other circumstance.

Whether the journeys you take are from Wisconsin to Sri Lanka or from "I can't" to "I can," I hope that the "postcards" in this book enliven the possibilities within your imagination while the "pearls" embolden your life at home in new and challenging ways.

Gina Greenlee
Hartford, Connecticut
February 2008

TIME TRAVEL

We do not know the true value of our moments
until they have undergone the test of memory.

Georges Duhamel

 From a small treasure box, a friend revealed more than a dozen postcards I had mailed to her from around the world. "I appreciated receiving these," she said. "They're special." I examined each card's photo, description, postmark and my handwritten missive. This tiny feast of the senses transported me back to moments in time with a visceral intensity I had not experienced when revisiting photo albums or journals.

I recalled when I first rounded the west gate to India's Taj Mahal. My Taj guide had taken his time to wind through the history of the building's construction, stopping every third yard to dramatize what he considered a noteworthy fact. My expectations sank with each superlative reference. I thought, *It can't be all that.*

My guide stopped just before the gate to put the finishing touch on his prologue. With a flourish akin to the doorman at a five-star hotel, he ushered me through the thick wooden doors. Then he stepped aside and waited for my reaction. "*Oh. My. God,*" was all I managed to say over and over again.

Mammoth and marble white, imposing yet elegant and accessible, the Taj wasn't architecture merely to be observed or entered like an office building. Rather, she was a coquette beckoning from a distance. And, she insisted on a slow flirtation along the quarter mile fore garden and the rectangular pool that reflected her image. I had come to see; I left bewitched.

As I returned the postcards to my friend I thought, *I wish I had sent these to myself.* Now I do.

Cherishing our own memories is as important as sharing them with others.

AWE

It's good to have an end to journey toward;
but it is the journey that matters, in the end.

Ursula LeGuin

 The last stop on my northern India itinerary was Agra, the home of the Taj Mahal. During my trip, locals and tourists alike asked me if I had seen it. "No," I said, "but I'm headed that way."

When I asked for a preview, "indescribable" was all they'd say. *It's just a building,* I thought. As I cleared the west gate of this architectural testimony of a man's eternal devotion to a woman, I saw it and froze in awe.

Though there's nothing to do in Agra except visit the Taj Mahal, I went back. Five times. I shot eight rolls of film: at sunrise, sunset, and with wide angle and telephoto lenses. I captured the Taj's mirror image in the reflecting pool that rests along the front entrance of the gardens, and at multiple angles through pink mist on a foggy morning, convinced I had wasted film. Instead, of more than 100 pictures I'd taken, the only shot of the monument that I framed emerged from that mist – the Taj cloaked in a mysterious haze of mauve.

I wrote to my friends and family back in the United States: "If it is possible to fall in love with a building, then that is my relationship to the Taj Mahal."

❧

When was the last time you allowed love to take you by surprise?

UNCOMMON GROUND

There is nowhere you can go and only be with people who are like you. Give it up.

Bernice Johnson Reagon

I had been up for an hour on Christmas morning before I realized, *Today's my birthday.* I was in Bikaner, a desert town in northern India. Without the usual holiday clues such as decorated trees and twinkling lights, I had forgotten it. As I rode in a motorized tri-shaw, relaxed into a trance by the desert images speeding past me, I remembered. Months earlier, I had arranged to distinguish my birthday with a camel safari.

My guide, Vijay, and I rode for hours as men waved and children ran alongside yelling, "Hello!" At one stop, the children pointed to my head and giggled, fascinated by the kinky texture of my hair. I moved toward them and bent down so they could touch it. They backed away squealing with laughter until one brave youth edged toward me, his index finger extended ET-style.

Other than vocabulary such as "lunch" and "bathroom, madam?" Vijay and I did not exchange words. He spoke Hindi and Urdu, and I spoke English. Yet we engaged a lexicon of smiles, shared silences and international charades. When Vijay made two fists then drew them sharply toward his collar bone, that meant "hold onto the camel reins;" when I rubbed my belly, that showed my appreciation for the amazing lunch cooked by two women who seemed to appear from nowhere, in the middle of the desert, hauling pots and pans.

At the end of the safari, Vijay treated me to a tour of his home – four sandstone dwellings with straw roofs. An area he called "room" was bare except for one straw cot covered with a spread and accented with decorative fabric overhead. Two adjacent walls held pictures of Hindu gods and goddesses, maharajahs and a black and white military group photo in which Vijay pointed to a younger version of himself.

As I waited for the tri-shaw that would take me back to my hotel, the children in Vijay's family gathered around me. They lifted the camera that hung around my neck toward my face and said, "You click! You click!" then scrambled to assemble themselves opposite the lens in a tableau of farewell.

***

Even when words fail us, our intent to understand and be understood spurs us to speak through the expanse of our senses and the integrity of our hearts.

FEAR

I've been absolutely terrified every moment of my life and I've never let it keep me from doing a single thing that I wanted to do.

Georgia O'Keeffe

 India had overwhelmed me by the time I reached Jaipur. I had received copious attention from men who offered to keep my company. Though I never felt threatened by their overtures, it exhausted me to fend them off.

I wanted to stroll the streets of the Pink City – nicknamed for the hue of its old buildings – but I couldn't muster the fortitude to venture beyond my room. I believed, though, that if I did not spend at least one day without a guide, wandering the bazaars and dining away from my hotel, that choice would become a metaphor for the rest of my life.

That's when I summoned the force of my native Manhattan: I encased myself in an invisible bubble and marched out. Again, the men persisted: "Hello! Where are you from? Nairobi? Jamaica? Can I walk with you? Where are you going?"

I didn't know where I was going. It was fun to meander with no planned destination, to flow with, not dictate the adventure. With purposeful body language, I kept walking, allowing the current of the city to carry me, moving beyond my fear by literally stepping into it.

Bulls roamed the arid streets, their formidable horns ensuring them a respectful berth. Motor scooters, cars, camel-drawn carts and monkeys queued at the few stoplights while waiting for the green. Sun-baked women, swathed in fluorescent silks, balanced the equivalent of their body weight in baskets of food on their heads. The aroma of street-baked sweets, incense and cow dung spiced the air.

And, as men with time on their hands approached me with curiosity about my life across the oceans, I felt as if I had sprinted through an open field with the wind at my back.

※

Do your fears warn of external dangers?
Or, are they the kind that keep you from becoming more of your true self?

CLARITY

Nobody can give you wiser advice than yourself.

Cicero

 As I walked down the streets of Jaipur, India, a tri-shaw driver, who introduced himself as "Indian Johnny," offered his services. "I don't want to ride," I told him. "I want to walk."

Johnny insisted that he would take me wherever I wanted to go and wait while I dined and shopped – "all for a good price." He wouldn't let up and slowly tracked my pace.

It was important for me to walk and not allow fear to prevent me from fully experiencing India. To communicate that to Johnny would have been a waste of time. But "no" didn't sway him either. Feeling worn down, I told him I'd ride with him to the main bazaar and afterward, I would be on my own.

After the usual questions – "Do you travel alone?" "Are you married?" "Do you have children?" – Johnny, who called his ride the "Chapati Express," said that he had "many friends in America." All were women whom he had met during their travels in Jaipur, he explained. According to Johnny, many were interested in his sexual favors. On the heels of this revelation came his attempt to steer our conversation toward carnal matters.

I hoped that by focusing the talk on the city I could make it to the bazaar without further hassle. But Johnny would not relent. His overtures became more explicit. So, I unleashed my native New Yorker in a tirade flammable enough to singe most people's eyebrows. Johnny didn't flinch. "Some women are interested," he said, shrugging. "You don't know. So you must ask."

∽≫∾

Honoring your own boundaries
is the clearest message to others to honor them, too.

THE RULES

If you obey all the rules, you miss all the fun.
                                        Katharine Hepburn

Heavy into shopping at the markets in Jaipur, I realized I was low on cash. It wasn't a bargaining ploy – $30 worth of rupees was all I had left. Because my hotel was nearby, I told the proprietors I'd exchange money and return to the shop to complete my transaction.

"No problem, Madam," one of the shopkeepers said. "We will go with you."

As the men traded animated sentences in Hindi, I thought, *You'll go with me? What does that mean?*

One man turned to me and said, "Just one moment," as another vanished into the back of the store. When the men motioned me outside, the disappearing man had reappeared with a motorbike, which turned my suspicion into excitement.

As we zipped through the cow-brimmed tangle of Jaipur's swarming streets, I no longer wanted to keep India at arm's length – from the window of a train or the bubble of a private car – as I had at the start of my trip. Our bike zigzagged through the dusty pink swirl, which at its center, staged a carnival of the senses for which I now wanted a front row seat.

Yes, Mama told me not to accept rides from strange men. And later that day as dusk approached, I declined an invitation from a man on a motorbike who offered me a ride to a "sacred" mountain. In one instance, I followed my mother's rule; in the other, I did not. The difference between the two? Context – enlightened by common sense.

❦

Some rules are made to be broken.
Even Mama's.

BREAKOUT

And the trouble is, if you don't risk anything, you risk even more.

Erica Jong

 Marita, a 63-year-old college professor, describes her "journey to discovering how to explore the world on my own."

"I am not a solitary person. As the mother of four children, wife of 37 years, grandmother, daughter, sister, friend, teacher, activist and volunteer, there have been few times in my life when I have done anything alone. And, for the most part, I have loved it that way. Although there have been moments when I have longed for a few minutes of alone time, it never entered my mind to sightsee or travel without someone by my side to share it with.

"However, since returning to school in my 40s, and becoming what is referred to as a 'professional,' I found myself traveling all over the country to attend conferences. For years, my idea of conference attendance was to arrive early enough to check into the hotel before the first session, and then head for the plane the minute the conference ended. The locale was irrelevant to me except to note that someday I might like to return 'for fun' which, of course, meant not by myself.

"One of our sons and his wife were taking a trip to Chicago. He called and asked if I had been there and, if so, what would I recommend they see? I told him I had been to Chicago at least twice in the previous 10 years but – and I realized this for the first time – I had never seen anything more than the inside of a hotel!

"I suppose this should have occurred to me sometime during my travels, but it hadn't. I decided that in the future, anytime I traveled to a new city, I would see at least one thing to help me to get to know it better."

❧

Change happens in increments.
What "one thing" can you do today to take a step toward lasting change?

EXPLORE

You are destined to fly but that cocoon has to go.
                                                    Nellie Morton

Marita writes, "A few months after my 'I-travel-but-I-really-don't' epiphany when talking to my son, I was scheduled to attend a conference in New Orleans. How fortunate I was to have made the commitment prior to this trip to explore new conference cities on my own.

"I arrived in New Orleans just 24 hours before the conference began. I spent the first afternoon by myself, walking around the French Quarter, stopping for a bite to eat in a café where I sat at a window seat to watch the world go by. I strolled in and out of shops, buying local cookbooks for my son the chef, and trinkets for my granddaughters. The next morning I walked to Riverfront Park and just allowed myself to get a feel for the city.

"The conference ended Sunday at noon, so I signed up for a bus tour of the area, including a stop at Evergreen Plantation and Laura Plantation. On the tour, I was fortunate to meet two women from Massachusetts, one with a digital camera. After the tour, the three of us had a wonderful dinner in the French Quarter."

❧

Put "explore" on today's to-do list: make reservations;
walk somewhere with your shoes off; say "yes" to that open invitation.

NEW VISTAS

*When I dare to be powerful – to use my strength in the service of my
vision, then it becomes less and less important whether I am afraid.*

Audre Lorde

 "When I was 20 years old," writes Marita, "I became a VISTA
Volunteer (Volunteers in Service to America) at a time when doing
so required a six-week training program. Because I participated in
the first class to serve on Indian reservations, my training, and then my year of
service, took place in Montana.

"Having grown up in a working class family and having attended a community
college, I had never traveled, and certainly had never been on a plane. I vividly
remember both the terror and the thrill of getting off the plane and realizing I
did not know anyone within 2,000 miles!

"My sister told me that she never could have done such a thing because she
would have been too afraid. She didn't understand how afraid I was even
though I told her. Perhaps it was back then that I learned that fear would not
stop me when there was hope of something worthwhile at the other end.

"That experience gave me a new sense of who I was as a person. Years later,
attending professional conferences all over the country was no big deal for me.
I was able to get on a plane, change planes and regroup after missing planes. I
could find lost luggage and make my way to hotels in a strange place without
panicking or stressing beyond the point of being able to deal with such situations.

"Although my family and friends have always seen me as self-confident and
able to handle most anything, that was never the way I viewed myself. Just the
act of traveling solo taught me I was more capable than I had believed myself
to be."

*What do you believe about who you are? About your capabilities?
When was the last time you trusted yourself enough to test them?*

BRING IT ON

Don't play for safety – it's the most dangerous thing in the world.
Hugh Walpole

 I was freelance writing for a newspaper that asked me to participate in an orienteering event, then write about my experience for the annual outdoor issue of its Sunday magazine.

Orienteering's purpose: navigate unfamiliar terrain using a topographic map and a compass to find sequential checkpoints or "controls" along a course, and return to the finish in the shortest elapsed time. The route between controls is unspecified, determined by the orienteer.

I wanted the byline but I didn't relish getting lost in the woods. I'm native to Manhattan; put me on the subway, blindfold me, spin me three times and, without breaking a nail, I'll get you from South Ferry to the Bronx faster than you can say, "Yankee Stadium." Turn me loose in the woods with something called a "topo" map and a compass, and you've got Jack London kind of trouble.

At the event's official start – a reservoir near my home – I got lost almost immediately. Into my second hour, I had only reached the third of 10 controls. As I sought to re-establish my bearings, I emerged from the woods dazed, a mere shell of the woman I was at the start.

En route to the eighth control I met another orienteer traveling at a nice clip. As we chatted, he didn't discourage me from using him as an "illegal" guide. Sheepishly, though with monumental relief, I walked with him to the finish.

My lifelong challenge with transporting myself from point A to point B in unfamiliar surroundings has always disturbed me. It feels rooted in fear of isolation and loss of control, incapacitating whatever logic, experience and instinct I usually draw from to solve problems.

Still, orienteering did not improve my directional skills. I came in dead last. But rather than break down in tears, as I had in the past on the shoulder of many a highway, I'd finally reached a point where I could tolerate, laugh at and rebound from my imperfections.

❧

If we never challenge our shortcomings,
we ensure that they remain our Achilles' heel.

IT'S TIME

Life shrinks or expands in proportion to one's courage.

Anaïs Nin

 Growing up in the Northeast United States, I've heard much about Martha's Vineyard, Nantucket, and "The Cape." Despite accolades for these areas from everyone I knew from New York to Maine, I had no interest in visiting them. But after living in Connecticut for several years, I decided I was too close not to visit.

When I asked my native New England friends for travel advice, it was only after they sprawled maps, detailed highway routes, ferry schedules and bed and breakfast locations did I become aware of the true source of my hesitance: logistics – especially the notorious highway drive from central Connecticut to the ferry landing in Woods Hole, Massachusetts. On a good day, it takes three hours. I learned how to drive later in life, am directionally challenged and easily overwhelmed by busy highways. The trip was unthinkable.

I confided my concerns in a friend who suggested a AAA bus trip. I had been a AAA member for as long as I'd been a driver. The agency was a godsend when my car had stalled more than once, but I had yet to take advantage of its travel services.

AAA offered several day trips to the famous tourist region, and required no more of me than showing up and boarding a bus. What a relief! Had I not addressed my fears, I doubt I would ever have gone.

❦

Name the fears that are holding you back.
It's the equivalent of flooding the boogeyman with light.

POSSIBILITIES

If we all did the things we are capable of doing,
we would literally astound ourselves.

Thomas Edison

 On day 13 of a 14-day trip across Morocco – from the Atlantic Ocean through the Cedar Forest and the Atlas Mountains, past oasis-cradled kasbahs and the velvety dunes of the eastern Sahara – in Marrakech I changed into dirhams the last of the American dollars I brought with me to tip my guide.

Rain drizzled, the sky grayed and I was dragging physically and emotionally, as I tend to do at the close of an extended, overseas journey: the adventure is near its end and the impending obligations of real life crowd my thoughts and siphon my energy. Also, I had planned to walk across the city to a Vietnamese restaurant I read about in a guidebook and, as usual, I was anxious about getting lost. When I approached the moneychanger, my defenses were down.

As I silently slipped the bills through the slot, the moneychanger asked me in French if the equivalent of $40 was all I wanted. Without thinking I said, *"Oui. Je retourne aux Etats-Unis demain"* – I'm returning to the United States tomorrow. I was surprised at how effortlessly the words tumbled from my lips without the usual puttering translation inside my head, a lingering habit from my college language study.

I surprised the moneychanger, too, because he remarked on the high quality of my French. When next he launched into questions about my life back home, the pressure mounted and my self-consciousness returned. Though I longed to converse with him, I couldn't keep up. I wished he would stop talking in French and finish our transaction.

But on a day that had begun as a downer, I felt buoyed as I tucked my 400 dirham in my money belt. And for the first time in 20 years, I believed that I could be fluent in another language.

❧

It is our beliefs, more than our experiences, that determine
life's possibilities.

TRUE ADVENTURE

Courage is the power to let go of the familiar.
                                        Raymond Lindquist

 I traveled solo to Greece, Turkey and Paris on a trip sponsored by a college near my home. The itinerary was open during two days in Paris, where I could easily access the sites I wanted to visit by riding *le métro* except that I had to rely on French language signage.

I'm great with navigating subways in English. In French, I was anxious about getting lost. But I did not want to spend one second in the City of Lights in my hotel room beyond what was required to sleep and shower. So, off I went to *Le Bureau de Change* to swap dollars for francs. There I bumped into eight women from the larger group with which I was traveling.

I learned that their itinerary was identical to my own: *Notre Dame, Sacre Cour,* the *Louvre* and *Montemarte*, among other popular sights. I was dying to go with them. So, I was thrilled to accept their offer to join their group because I didn't want to ask; I was afraid they would say, "No."

My childhood was filled with an endless string of "nos" from family members who lacked the emotional skills to respond to my need for nurturing, companionship and affection. In my adult life, that translated into staunch independence and unwillingness to take emotional risks. Though I had traveled far in the physical world, my emotional journeys had not kept pace.

For all the opportunities that solo travel creates for me to affirm and expand my independence, it creates equal opportunity to acknowledge and act on my need for relationship with others.

❧

Embrace those parts of yourself that you've skillfully avoided until now.
That's your true adventure.

MY WAY

If you can't be direct, why be?
Lily Tomlin

In Paris, one morning I spontaneously joined a group of women whose sightseeing plans mirrored my own.

Our last stop before dinner was the *Louvre*. The museum is half price on Sunday and after 3 p.m. on other days. Just before 2 p.m., we arrived at the *Carrousel du Louvre* mall, an underground museum entrance. Surrounding us were international chain stores, many of which occupy most American malls. Because we had an hour before half-price admission, most of the women considered this an opportunity to shop.

It was April, it was Paris and shopping below ground at The Tie Rack was not on my itinerary. Instead, I was close enough to walk to *Jardin des Tuileries* at *la Place de la Concorde* and from there shoot that famous perspective picture of the *Arc de Triomphe* at the head of the *Champs-Elysées*.

My destination was close but in native New Yorker terms, meaning I would have to practically run through the streets of Paris to take my picture so I could return to the *Louvre* within the hour.

One woman asked to join me. I didn't want to say, "No." She had been among the group of travelers who welcomed me on their day tour of the city. However, to answer "Yes," as though this were going to be a leisurely stroll, would have been disingenuous.

I was on a mission.

Before my trip, friends encouraged me to take this photograph. But there was much to cram into two days. What a nice surprise then, when this "free" hour opened up. I could squeeze in the photo after all.

I explained the mission and detailed the strategy to my would-be companion: return to the *Louvre* by 3 p.m. to allow time to visit key paintings before meeting the group for dinner. If she could walk Manhattan style then she was most welcome. It turns out, her company was a bonus: she photographed me in the shot. Later, we laughed about how I "dragged" her through the streets of Paris.

❦

Be tactful. Be polite. But be yourself.

DEEP AND WIDE

Never be afraid to sit awhile and think.
                              Lorraine Hansberry

 Each extraordinary wing of the *Louvre* – the Richelieu, Sully, and Denon – houses collections within eight departments: Asian; Egyptian; Greek and Roman antiquities; Islamic Art; sculpture; decorative arts; paintings; and prints and drawings.

The three wings are laid out like spokes on a wheel. Because the entrance and exit of each wing are one and the same and lie at the museum's center, visitors can't travel from one to the other without retracing their steps: they must exit a wing at the hub and then enter a new wing from the same point. Not a big deal, unless it is the day before Easter Sunday when thousands of international visitors are in town to worship at *Notre Dame* and are funneling through the museum's wings at the same time.

I have a friend who, on one of her trips to Paris, spent 10 consecutive hours alone in the *Louvre*. Her time at the museum was deep. For me, the pedestrian equivalent of a backup on the entrance ramp to the George Washington Bridge required my time at the *Louvre* to be wide. I didn't have 10 hours to devote to the museum and I didn't want to spend the two I did have admiring only one painting.

It took me 90 minutes to visit only five pieces of art: *Venus de Milo*, *Mona Lisa*, *Winged Victory*, *Whistler's Mother* and Michelangelo's *Slaves*.

Realistic about how much time it would take to return to my hotel in *Saint-Germain-des-Prés* and prepare for dinner, I allowed myself a sliver of deep within the expanse of wide: for half an hour I contented myself on a bench opposite a painting by William Adolphe Bouguereau – one of my favorite artists – and took a breather from the crowd.

Stop. And find a pocket of peace.

KNOW HOW

Deal with yourself as an individual worthy of respect and make everyone else deal with you the same way.

Nikki Giovanni

Frances, a 69-year-old retired real estate administrator, writes about her most challenging solo travel experience.

"I traveled solo to Spain when I was 66 years old. I signed on for a project that would require me to speak with Spaniards who were brushing up on their conversational English. After two weeks, I was going to fly from Madrid to Barcelona but one of the Spaniards was driving there so I rode with him.

"My problem was that by accepting this ride I would arrive one day ahead of my hotel reservation. The man I drove to Barcelona with spoke little English. I spoke no Spanish, so he called the hotel for me to see if I could arrive a day early. The manager said they were completely booked. My Spanish friend made an impromptu reservation for me by a *pensione* for one night. This seemed fine. When we arrived in Barcelona, we said good-bye; then I took a taxi to the *pensione*.

"When I saw the building and surrounding area I knew I could not stay in this place. The taxi driver agreed with me. I told him to take me to the hotel where I had a reservation starting the next day.

"It was the beautiful, four-star Colon Hotel. I went inside and spoke to the night manager. He said he was sorry but no rooms were available. I worked for a real estate developer in New York City that owned hotels so I knew that first class establishments always have a room or two, usually a penthouse or executive suite that has not been booked. I asked to speak to the general manager. He came to meet me and looked me up and down; I did not look my best. I explained my situation and suggested that they must have one room – no matter how expensive – that they could give me. He checked the bookings again and said "Yes," for the night he had an executive suite. In the morning after breakfast they would move me into my original room.

"That night was spent in luxury. The room overlooked the front of the hotel, which was in a square, and faced a most beautiful cathedral across the street. The next day I was moved to a small room in the back of the hotel at a much lesser rate."

Who you know only gets you in the door;
what you know gets you the keys to the house.

AS IT COMES

The good traveler has the gift of surprise.
William Somerset Maugham

 Lynn, a 58-year-old writer, writes, "I've been vacationing solo since my marriage ended in the '70s. I was 32 before I ever had a chance to travel alone or sleep one night away from a family member.

"One year in the '80s, I drove to Florida with only the barest itinerary. I had an aunt there and I visited her for two days, but the rest of the time I explored St. Augustine and Daytona, stopping wherever I felt like it. That's usually how I do it. I have a general target but I do whatever I want before and after that, almost never planning hotels, motels or any stops ahead.

"Sometimes I'll sit with a guidebook in a restaurant and make decisions as the spirit moves me. Not planning can be dicey at times like when I had to drive until 4 a.m. to find a motel. Other times, I've had to sleep in my car because I couldn't find a place to stop, though that's rare.

"For my cross-country trip, the 'target' was seeing my daughter perform in Oregon. On that driving trip, I kept myself occupied by making audiotapes as I traveled, and I stopped regularly along the roadside to pick up rocks and take close-up pictures of flowers."

❧

Sometimes we just have to wing it.

MY TURN

Whatever good there is to get
get it and feel good

Ntozake Shange (from Get it and Feel Good)

 Beth, a 49-year-old hair salon owner, traveled solo for the first time to Holland and Belgium.

"During the experience I was a bit nervous," Beth writes, "but that faded quickly when I realized how easy it was. I chose countries that spoke a lot of English and had well-developed mass transit systems. I made reservations at accommodations beforehand so I didn't have to worry about where to lay my head. I felt liberated, free, and totally in love with doing what I wanted, when I wanted and where I wanted. I ate when I pleased, talked to whom I pleased and enjoyed the ability to be totally self-absorbed.

"I waited this long to take my first solo trip because I had never asked for my needs to be met. I always thought somebody else's needs came first. I don't think the word 'selfish' is negative – not in total. Selfish is taking care of self, not unresponsiveness to others."

You're next.

NEW TERRITORY

I'm trying to think of the last time that I just said,
"What the hell" and did something crazy.

Jennifer Aniston

Chelsey, a 20-year old prep cook in a health food restaurant, recalls her first solo trip.

"I flew from Connecticut to Montana where I stayed for a week. I had just turned 19. A friend of mine knew someone there who had an apartment. I thought it was pretty cool that this guy was willing to let me stay in his place, even though we'd never met. I guess having a mutual friend was enough for him to trust me in his apartment and for me to trust that I'd be safe there.

"The morning of my flight, I was nervous. I had never flown alone before. My Mom offered to stay with me until I got through the security check. It was reassuring to have her along. Once I got to my gate, I felt a lot better. I was through the hard part: it was unbelievably difficult at 5:30 on a Sunday morning to take off my shoes, belt and coat while carrying a duffel bag stuffed with a week's worth of clothing and not drop anything.

"I switched planes in St. Paul, Minnesota. I made sure to call my Mom every chance I got. I'm the fifth of seven kids in a close family. We all live in the same town, and rarely do we go more than three days without seeing each other. For me to spend a week on the other side of the country was a little frightening.

"My week in Montana passed quickly. I went shopping, to museums, took lots of pictures, and drank lots of hot chocolate. I also discovered my new obsession at The Leaf and Bean Coffee House – a drink called the Bozeman's Big Apple (similar to a Caramel Apple Cider at Starbucks but much better).

"The people in Montana were the nicest I'd ever met. Every shop owner wanted to talk to me, and not just the 'Hi, how are you today?' you get at the register. It was the kind of talk that started with 'Boy, you sure have a funny accent. Where 'bouts are you from?' (I'd like to point out that I do not have an accent. I'm from New England, where everyone talks like they need to blow their nose, but I wouldn't consider it an accent. Montanans, however, have the most musical speech I'd ever heard. I could move there just to hear them talk.)"

⸎

In the changing weather of life, rather than drift with the
currents or be cast about in storms, be the wind at your own back.

TEST FLIGHT

Monotony is the awful reward of the careful.

A.G. Buckham

Chelsey writes about her airport experience after spending a week in Montana.

"After checking in at a three-gate airport in Montana, I flew to the largest airport I'd ever seen. I was back in St. Paul, but this time I wasn't lucky enough to have my connecting flight be two gates down. I had to cross the whole airport, and I didn't have much time to do it.

"I was terrified that I would miss my flight and be stuck in Minnesota. One of the lessons my Mom worked so hard to teach me and my brothers and sisters was to always know where you are and what's around you, like where the nearest exit is. With this in mind, I found an airport map. With my finger, I traced the route I would have to take to get from the 'you are here' star to my gate. It looked like I had to go as far as possible from where I was standing. I took off running, slinging my duffle over my head as I went, and tried my hardest not to knock into anyone. I ran past people standing still on the moving sidewalks. It took me a full 15 minutes to get to my gate.

"I arrived at my gate out of breath and with 10 minutes to spare. I called my Mom again to let her know I was on my way. My hands were shaking as I dialed her number. I slept the rest of the flight, and my Mom met me at the airport and brought me home.

"I think this first solo trip gave me the confidence to travel solo again. I'd never gone anywhere by myself or been that far from home. To do both in one trip was scary and exciting at the same time. The fact that nothing went wrong, I took care of myself for a week and made it home alive, makes me think I can do it again, anytime I want."

❧

Adventure, opportunity and reward extend beyond our field of vision, and are made known to us only when we test our wings.

THE MIDDLE WAY

The really idle man gets nowhere.
The perpetually busy man does not get much further.

Sir Heneage Ogilvie

 I was in marathon training during my first visit to Greece. When I discovered that The National Garden was walking distance from my hotel in Athens, I decided to go there for a morning run. I ran through sections with lovely flowers and strolling families. But the truncated, curvy paths caused me concern for pedestrian collision.

In search of open space, I ran past the playground and landed in an area with different energy: all men, all milling not walking, with their hands inside the pockets of their long, stained raincoats.

Rather than risk running into creepier territory, I slowed my run to a walk toward the nearest exit. One man walked several feet behind me but kept pace as he muttered to himself. When I turned to check his proximity, he addressed me loudly in Greek. I put my hand up and yelled, "Stop!" Though my command was in English, my tone and body language were international. He lunged toward me anyway and I bolted.

I wanted to train for my race but not at the expense of my safety. So I ditched the garden and ran through the neighborhood of my hotel along the densely trafficked avenue leading to the Parthenon.

For the next two days, I wore a hole in that patch of street. I intended to run, if not for my training, then to ensure that an isolated incident did not mushroom into debilitating fear.

For me, having routinely lived life's extremes, this approach was inaugural. In the past, I would have taken an either/or stance: *either* run risky *or* not at all. But I triumphed in Athens the day I chose balance by choosing the middle way.

Forget black and white and try on gray. In hair color, wardrobe or life choices, it may feel more enlivening than you imagine.

EXPANSION

We travel, initially, to lose ourselves; and we travel,
next, to find ourselves.

Pico Iyer

 On my way back to my hotel from London's Piccadilly Circus, I met a charming woman on the Underground. A retired Air Force intelligence officer, she had lived all over the world during her career. She spoke several languages and was living in Atlanta where she was part of an expatriate club that convened once per month for cultural gatherings that reflected the international experience of its members. Membership qualifications required fluency in at least two languages, and two consecutive years of expatriatism.

After we exchanged farewells, two distinct feelings swept over me: hope and despair. Hope, because I had met a living role model for the life I had been craving but didn't know how to create – aligning earning power, passion and geographic mobility. Despair, because I felt stuck in my life situation.

Later, memories of our conversation inspired me to draw up a pact with myself: I vowed that my time in London would be more than a weeklong getaway. Rather, my England vacation would mark the beginning of a more authentic life. And, once back home, I would use the experience as a metaphor to transform thought energy into tangible expression. I called it "The London Life Expansion Pact."

I read my Pact every day for six months. Two years later, I stumbled across it and was astounded by how dramatically my life had changed. I had resigned my full-time job to travel around the world, launched a freelance journalism career with a regular column in Connecticut's largest newspaper, and begun the draft of this book.

☞

When we write down our dreams,
we transform what we imagine into reality.

SOMETHING MORE

*Only by learning to live in harmony with your contradictions
can you keep it all afloat.*

Audre Lorde

 In 1992, I spent two weeks as an educational lecturer aboard a cruise ship that was sailing throughout the Caribbean. I was in my early 30s and was one of a handful of solo women travelers among mostly senior couples. The ship's all-male crew treated my arrival in the dining room like a national holiday.

The sommelier for my dinner table was particularly attentive. I enjoyed flirting with him – an activity I rarely engage in unless I'm seriously interested in a man. But I was on vacation and it seemed like harmless fun.

One evening, the sommelier arranged for us to meet in an empty cabin. Only as we sat on the edge of a single twin bed did I fully grasp the scenario and then retreat to my stateroom. What was I thinking? This wasn't my style. Besides, I had a lover back home.

I recalled how my lover of six months boasted that several women at his job found him attractive. While lavishing me with attention, he also made it clear that he had other options. What was going on at sea was that I wanted to prove – if only to myself – that I also had options. So, on the eve of disembarkation, I decided to visit the sommelier in his quarters. I enjoyed nothing about that encounter, nor did it bolster my esteem.

After yielding to attention from strange men to compensate for lack of respect back home, I realized that the something more I wanted from my lover was the something I would first have to give to myself.

❧

What we seek when we wander usually leads us back home.

ROMANCE

Romance is the glamour that turns the dust of every day life into a golden haze.

Amanda Cross

 My expectations got the better of me as I assumed that an evening in San Marco Square in Venice, Italy, was akin to *you've seen one piazza, you've seen them all* – an immense, open space surrounded by magnificently old and breathtaking buildings.

I was on a two-week, whirlwind mega tour – *if it's Tuesday, it must be Sorrento* – scheduled to visit every major region between Sicily and the Swiss border in northern Italy. For 14 days I never laid my head in one place for more than two nights. I was tired, jaded and tempted to spend my only night in Venice in my hotel bed. Fortunately for me, I made new acquaintances on my tour who assured me that would not be happening.

During the day, San Marco Square buzzed with the energy of tourists who took photos and rode water taxis, sampled gelato and visited the bell tower and cathedral. Among other tourist traditions, I met my new friends for Bellinis – a champagne and peach nectar cocktail – at the world famous Harry's Bar. It was fun.

But when night settled on San Marco, it cloaked the square in a silence penetrated only by the echo of violin strings from the outdoor orchestral music cafés. It was then that Venice lived up to its reputation as a city of magic and romance.

At Florian's, the white linen canopies stirred and the famous flocks of pigeons slept as the evening air cooled the square. Its vastness was made intimate with notes from Pachelbel, Ravel and Vivaldi, the tinkling of glass and appreciative bursts of applause.

Positioned at a table between the melodious strings and stream of *passeggiare* – the after-dinner stroll that begins every evening in Italy at 9 – I toasted the night's delights and exchanged satisfied smiles and glances with everyone around the table.

The clock hands swept too swiftly, and our check arrived too soon, as the promise of an early rise brought mood, moonlight and music to an end.

～⁂～

Feeling lonely? Wish you had a special someone to help fill the void? Reconsider your definition of romance, reconnect to your passions and be swept away.

CHOICES

Don't be afraid your life will end; be afraid that it will never begin.
Grace Hansen

After years of procrastination, I booked a two-week vacation to Egypt scheduled for January 1998. In November 1997, terrorist snipers at Hatshepsut's temple in Luxor killed 58 tourists, two police officers, and two Egyptian civilians before being killed by authorities. In the days following the news report of the attack, all my colleagues said, "You're going to cancel, right?"

Thousands of international tourists had already done so, setting off a tourism drought in Egypt. The travel company I had signed on with offered refunds, alternative destinations, and rebooking for the following year. In addition to those options, the company also decided to run the original January trip. Of the 141 travelers initially booked, 35 flew to Egypt.

I was one of them.

Why did I go? First, the logical reasons: the Egyptian government had heightened security measures across the country, especially at tourist attractions, and had cracked down on known terrorist groups. I learned that those responsible for the attack were an isolated, disorganized band of militants. Also, I reasoned that my safety would be no more guaranteed if I postponed my trip to the following year or the year after that.

Now, the reasons that matter most: Even if I hadn't planned to visit Egypt, hanging out in Hartford, Chicago or Boston wouldn't provide immunity against death. My time will come even if I never leave my living room. But in November 1997, I became the clearest I've ever been about how I choose to live.

~~~

Much of our lives consists of a series of choices over which we have absolute control.

LEAP

There is a time when we must firmly choose the course which we will follow or the endless drift of events will make the decision for us.

Herbert V. Prochnow

 In 1992, I moved to Singapore for a year. It was on behalf of an employer that allowed four weeks for me to pack up my house, car and possessions, and prepare emotionally to leave my home country.

I was barely out of my 20s when I moved to Singapore, tittering with excitement about the possibilities that awaited me, while also wondering if I was out of my mind. I owned two pieces of real estate – my home and a condo I rented. I adored my historic home, a 200-year old townhouse with a wrought iron spiral staircase, skylights, exposed brick and wood beams. I had always dreamed of owning a house like that. It reminded me of the West Village brownstones of my Manhattan childhood, except in the gentrifying Baltimore, Maryland, of 1991, it was affordable. It stunned even me, that less than a year after I'd bought it, I was letting it go.

I sold my car and rented my house – only because there wasn't enough time to sell it before I left. And though I worked for the same employer, I quit my stale stateside job. With the bulk of my possessions in storage, and one suitcase in hand, I boarded a plane headed for Southeast Asia not knowing what my fate would be a year later. Where would I live? Where would I be working? Who would I be working for? Also, other than my work responsibilities I knew only that when the jet landed I would stay at the Shangri-La Hotel. And, with the help of my new boss, I would have two weeks to arrange for a place to live. Until my Singapore move, I didn't know I had the capacity for that large a faith.

On the airplane, I breathed deeply and told myself that all I had to do for the next 24 hours was enjoy the flight. I trusted that by making it this far with hundreds of decisions behind me, I would figure out the rest as it came – one moment at a time.

❧

The notion of the perfect time is more than myth.
It's the ultimate self-delusion.

SOMETHING NEW

*One of the reasons people stop learning is that they
become less and less willing to risk failure.*

John W. Gardner

 I flew to Austin, Texas, to visit a college buddy I hadn't seen since we graduated 20 years earlier. After we caught up on our news, I asked if we could tour the galleries of Austin's thriving arts community.

During the weekend, my friend graciously drove me to different art enclaves around the city, including a strip of galleries on Congress Avenue, many containing potent "outsider" art. We wandered separately among the different sections of each gallery, indulging our own pace and individual tastes. At one location, I discovered the large-scale work of a nationally recognized metal sculptor. I've always wanted to work with big metal. And the striking sculptures by this artist and his students reconnected me to that yearning.

"Do you teach classes?" I asked a gallery representative on a whim. She said that the sculptor offered workshops four times a year. "And, they're lots of fun."

Feeling silly, I said, "I live in Connecticut."

"That's okay with us," she said. So, I signed the studio's mailing list.

The following summer, I received an e-mail invitation to a fall workshop scheduled almost a year to the day I had visited my college friend.

As I prepared for my Big Metal Weekend, the distance I would travel no longer seemed silly. It made a lot of sense. This workshop was a way for me to return to the creative dreams of my childhood. It was also a friendly reminder that I was overdue for something new.

*It's tempting to believe that a break from life's routine will only cause chaos.
But regimen does not ensure security. The only constant we can count on
is change.*

ALCHEMY

In the beginner's mind, there are many possibilities.
In the expert's mind, there are few.

Daisetsu Suzuki

 I spent a fall weekend learning how to sculpt metal at a cattle ranch west of Austin, Texas, called The Bunkhouse at Cypress Mill. During three, seven-hour days I pummeled and twisted metal with the help of hand tools and an oxygen-acetylene torch. The "shop" was set up outdoors where the sun, breeze and shade of the live oaks kept us company while we worked. I learned at least eight basic techniques of direct metal sculpture, including fusion, soldering, brazing and reticulation. The result was a hefty, handmade tomahawk.

My time on the ranch filled me with opportunities to feel artistic process in my body, to engage it in ways long forgotten in more than 13 years of working in corporate America, sitting in cubicles, crafting strategic plans and writing sales proposals.

The 350-acre ranch belied its pockets of fairytale settings such as a crystal clear swimming creek fed from an underground river nearby. My weekend was filled with warm walks to the creek canopied by lush cypress trees, and solitary strolls among the postcard stillness of lone horses and cows at pasture. It was filled with southern sensibilities, sitting around a dinner table – family style while passing bowls, sharing a break and telling jokes – feeling as if I belonged.

❧

To commune with your heart and soul, be willing to
go out of your mind.

TIME OUT

Longing is the soul's way of saying,
"I know you thought this was it, but it's not. Don't stop here."
Geneen Roth

 Beth went to Israel for the first time with congregants from her synagogue. One evening, the group was heavily negotiating its dinner venue. After several minutes, Beth's travel companions hadn't made a decision. She became antsy and took off to create a solo moment she had envisioned since the day the group visited the King David Hotel in Jerusalem.

"Nothing stands between me and my meals," Beth writes. "Besides, my soul needed some time with itself. I knew I wanted to go back to King David and this was my opportunity.

"Earlier when we visited the hotel, I thought the ambience was interesting: an open terrace in the back, a view of the old city and a three-piece music combo. When I went back for dinner, I asked the musicians to play my favorite song, 'My Funny Valentine,' and I slipped them a tip. It was my moment and my nicest meal in Israel."

❧

No moment is too small to claim.
Strung together, moments fashion a life.

BREAK AWAY

*Very often, a change of self is needed more
than a change of scene.*

Arthur Christopher Benson

 Kerry writes, "I spent most of one summer involved in other people's activities. But when I traveled with my parents and one of my sisters to Martha's Vineyard for a week, I finally figured out a way to be alone.

"At the end of one of the main streets in Vineyard Haven is a massage center. This street is usually crowded with tourists shopping for jewelry, books or Vineyard artwork. The center is on the second floor of a wood shingled building, next door to a gallery featuring crafts from around the world. The sidewalk ends at the massage center, causing most tourists to turn around. I took this as an invitation – no, as confirmation – that things could only get better. Inside the center, the cool conditioned air alone was enough to make me pay the owner.

"They scheduled me for the next day, just after lunch. It was great to say to my parents and my sister, 'I have plans. See you all later.' Surprise, surprise, they had plans, too. I was delighted that they didn't care.

"I could have cried the massage and solitude were so sweet. Just a few days ago, I found the business card to the center. They'll see me again this August and I will schedule my massage before I leave home."

Life's surprises are revealed to those who look.

JUST FOR ME

You need only claim the events of your life to make yourself yours.
Florida Scott-Maxwell

 Priscilla, a 61-year-old communications consultant and writer, describes the times she sought solo moments on the road.

"Being in a hotel room alone was especially wonderful when my kids were small. Also, I always visit art museums alone. And I love walking endlessly through foreign cities on my own, taking in the atmosphere.

"As part of a longer trip, I once sneaked into Paris from Brussels so I could spend time in the city alone. I had friends in Paris but I told them I was still in Belgium. I was 56 then. When I was 45, I went to London. I love that city, so I didn't contact anyone I knew so I could hit the streets on my own.

"When I take these trips I feel like I'm getting away with something. It's great to escape constant company, which I need to do periodically. However, if I had spent weeks alone, I don't think I would have liked that. I almost always travel on my own, visiting friends in various places but making sure I'm not committed to someone else's agenda."

❧

You've just been given the gift of a weekend to yourself. Family members are caring for your children and managing your house. You may not run errands, clean or catch up on your "to do" list. On your mark, get set, go!

THE GLAMOROUS LIFE

Freedom is never given; it is won.

A. Philip Randolph

 Mary, a 72-year-old author, has traveled solo for more than 30 years.

"From 1964 to 1994, my family was in Texas and I was in New York. So, I always traveled by motor home to see them. I'd wander, picking a different route each trip, exploring Florida one time, then Louisiana...

"As a teacher, I had summers off. I was an expert dawdler, sometimes driving only 60 miles a day, beach to beach. It was heaven. Especially after a stressful, busy time, there was nothing like the relief of turning the ignition key and saying, 'I'm outta here!'

"I got spoiled quickly. I loved having my own bed, my own clean bath, and nobody's noisy party next door. And I could rise at 4 a.m., fix breakfast – kitchen's always open! – or drive on if I wanted. Also, I liked my clothes hanging up, not folded in suitcases, my cosmetics always in a bathroom cabinet, and the freedom to stop as I pleased – to wait out bad weather, or just relax, read or watch TV. (By the way, what a hoot it is to pull off the road when it's jammed, sit and drink lemonade and watch people in regular cars steaming!)

"Also, I loved taking my animals with me. No more nightmares with cages and planes. Plus, they gave great security. A German shepherd sitting in a passenger seat assures a woman alone NO PROBLEMS! The ultimate luxury: to sleep when you're tired and eat when you're hungry, held to no one's timetable but your own.

"I started my RV travels at age 34 and quit at 64 when I moved to Florida. But I still drive a small motor home (class B) because I feel a vehicle is no use without a fridge, bed, and potty."

Is there a place you can go to break away for a little while? If you haven't yet built your tree house, it's never too late to start.

EPIPHANY

If you can bear it, the soles of our feet lead us to the feats of our souls.
Julia Cameron

I participated in a series of ropes courses at Boston University's Sargent Center for Outdoor Education in New Hampshire. I jumped from 70-foot bridges and zip-lined off of 60-foot parapets with the expectation that I would confront my fears and then apply what I'd learned as a model for transcending them.

One problem – I had only two memories from each course: the moment I jumped and the moment I landed. My free falls had been a blank. I had no recollection of confronting anything. No moments of staring down fear, no grand transcendence, either.

A few months earlier, I had begun to see a psychotherapist for the first time. When she used the phrases, "not being in your body" and "dissociation," she might as well have been speaking Cantonese. She told me, "With your childhood history of neglect and abuse, you had to leave your body. It was the only way to survive."

It wasn't until I careened from death defying heights 400 miles away from home, that I understood her meaning. And, though I could not have articulated it, deep down I knew that recovering a life suspended meant recovering my connection to my body.

❧

Let your body move. It will give voice to a language that can heal.

LUGGAGE

To wait for... or expect someone else to make my life richer or fuller or more satisfying, puts me in a constant state of suspension.

Kathleen Tierney Andrus

 I traveled solo for 25 years before my first encounter with lost luggage. Flagstaff, Arizona, was the departure city for my eight-day trek in the Grand Canyon. The fall nights were cool. The tour leader was picking me up first thing the next morning. I needed my gear.

Two other women were missing their luggage, too. As they sat on a bench and chatted, their husbands and I reported for lost luggage duty at the airline service counter.

Uh oh – the travel gods had favored me for a quarter century; why bother keeping track of a baggage claim check now?

My mind was flooded with the possibilities that lay ahead should my luggage not arrive in time for my departure to the Grand Canyon. I shared my concerns with the service representative who hypothesized that my duffel would be on the next flight to Flagstaff, dictated by airline protocol. It would likely arrive in two hours. Did I want it delivered to my hotel? Also, he suggested: "There's a shopping plaza walking distance from where you're staying. I've hiked the canyon before. Whatever you need for the trip you'll find there, but I doubt it will come to that."

I took a cab to the hotel. Without the responsibility of luggage, there seemed little point in going to my room. Instead, I relaxed with a sushi dinner and warm sake before checking in. Afterward, up in my room on the bed was my duffel.

Since then, I've held onto my baggage claim check like it was cash and I never pack anything I can't live without.

No matter how small, situations will arise that require us to be our own back up.

ROOM

Take care to get what you like or you will be forced to like what you get.
George Bernard Shaw

 On a hiking trip to the Grand Canyon, I asked the tour company to pair me with a roommate. I didn't want to pay the $300 single supplement – the fee that travel operators charge solo travelers to compensate for what they consider revenue lost on double-occupancy rates. The $300 fee was hefty enough to convince me that I could handle for one week whatever personality the Universe brought my way.

I got lucky. My roomie was a Ph.D. student on her first solo trip, who looked forward to sharing short-term living quarters. Both only children, we shared similar cohabitation values. Susan and I defied the misconceptions of the self-centered only child because we'd been well trained by our families to be sensitive to the domiciliary needs of others.

Another woman in our group of 10 solo travelers wasn't as fortunate. Her assigned roommate habitually transformed their shared bathroom into a 24-hour laundry. And, among other inconsiderate acts, left her undergarments soaking in the sink.

I took both roommate situations as signs to consider myself blessed, but vowed never to room with a stranger again.

❧

Make informed decisions about the company you keep.

DARE

It is not because things are difficult that we do not dare.
It is because we do not dare that things are difficult.

Seneca

 Susan, a 34-year-old doctoral student, writes, "I hadn't gone on a real vacation in several years and desperately needed one. No one I knew was in a position to take a trip, and I didn't want to wait any longer to start seeing the world, so I decided to go it alone. I went on a hiking tour of the Grand Canyon with a commercial travel company.

"At first, it was terrifying. I've never been daring, and I was taking a type of trip that was totally new to me with people I had never met before. But by the end of the trip, I felt incredibly liberated. Not only had I survived, but also, I had a wonderful time. And, I had set new boundaries for my life.

"Now, I no longer feel like I have to wait until I have a man in my life to start living. I can go to the places I want to go and see the things I want to see on my own schedule. I also learned that pushing past anxiety to try something new is worth it, and I have been much more adventurous since my trip."

❦

What is it time for you to brave?

NEW BEGINNINGS

The world is round and the place which may seem like the end may also be only the beginning.

Ivy Baker Priest

 Marita writes, "Traveling solo has given me confidence in my ability to face the unknown. It may sound crazy, but traveling to other parts of the country has given me more confidence to negotiate my way around my own little part of the world.

"Ten years ago when our son first started going to school in the city of Hartford when we lived in the suburbs, I was certain I would get lost. I was fearful to drive in the city because it had been so long since I had done so. Now I drive from Connecticut to Boston; Springfield, Massachusetts; and Queens with hardly a second thought. I still don't like driving in traffic, but the point is I do it.

"Solo travel has also taught me that it is OK to do things alone. Now I will go to Hartford Stage to see a play, even if there is no one willing or able to go with me. Not only do I do it, but also I am able to enjoy it. I am less self-conscious about eating alone in restaurants, something I don't ever remember doing before I traveled solo for business.

"I enjoy the wonder I feel walking around a new place and developing comfort with myself as a traveler that I have never had before. For those who have traveled by themselves since they were young, such experiences may be second nature; for me it is still an adventure.

"How fortunate I am that I began to take these steps before my husband died. I doubt I would have been able to begin this new way of being and doing after the devastation of such a loss."

❧

Develop the habit of initiating change.
You'll be better prepared for whatever comes your way.

PIONEER

A frontier is never a place; it is a time and a way of life.
Hal Borland

 Marita writes, "I just got back from Oakland, California, where I attended a conference for work. Never having been to Oakland, I decided to spend time before the conference getting to know the area around the hotel.

"I enjoyed discovering outdoor fresh food markets, two fabulous restaurants and It's a Grind coffee shop, all within easy walking distance of the hotel (even for someone with two relatively new artificial knees).

"The next morning, I checked my map to discover I was only about one half mile from Jack London Square, Oakland's waterfront area. I can't even describe the exhilaration of walking along the water early in the morning. I captured the beat of the city with my digital camera before most people were awake.

"By the time the conference began that evening I was able to tell newcomers to the city what they should absolutely see that was near the hotel. Many thanked me over the course of the conference for suggesting they take a walk by the water early in the morning. Not only did I enjoy a bit of Oakland, but I also got to share it with others who might not have taken the time to discover it.

"As someone who was convinced she could never enjoy sightseeing alone, I continue to be amazed at how taking time to explore the sights and sounds of a new place has enabled me to quiet my soul and enliven my heart. Perhaps that sounds a bit melodramatic, but these experiences have been transformative as I discover I can walk alone in the world without feeling lonely."

The best way to teach is how you live your life.

TABLE FOR ONE

When from our better selves we have too long
Been parted by the hurrying world, and droop,
Sick of its business, of its pleasures tired,
How gracious how benign, is Solitude.

William Wordsworth (from The Prelude)

 After a full day of interaction with clients and colleagues in Connecticut, I looked forward to a leisurely dinner at a local restaurant. As I stood at the door waiting to be seated, the host smiled at the couple ahead of me and asked, "Table for two?" He returned, approached me, and with little eye contact, said, "Just one?"

Once seated, I beckoned to the host and said, "Let me suggest that 'table for one' is more customer-friendly than '*just* one.'"

I was dining solo by choice, not default. I could have phoned several friends but I had been with people all day. I simply wanted to sit, sip wine and anticipate a meal at a favorite Indian restaurant.

I've been eating Indian food since I was 10 years old. I don't need a menu. By the time I arrive at the restaurant, my meal has been arranged on the banquet table of my imagination: hot *paratha* (flat bread), lightly salted and fried in *ghee* (homemade butter) to a delicate yet flaky perfection; a small steaming bowl of *mulligatawny* (lentil) soup; and a myriad of condiments such as tamarind chutney, hot cilantro chutney and chopped red onions.

Following this appetizer and served in a metal, oval dish is spicy *shag paneer* (spinach with homemade cheese). The red velvet curtain that brings this satisfying meal to its finale is a dessert called *golub jamun* (two sweetened balls of deep-fried cheese soaking in clear, warm syrup).

Bravo!

❦

The next time someone tries to make you feel bad about feeling good,
respond by continuing to live well.

ALONE TOGETHER

We decided it would be interesting to approach the music as a group solo.
Herbie Hancock

On day four of my weeklong, Grand Canyon hiking trip, I was en route to the Havasupai Reservation, the one place in the United States where a mule train delivers the mail daily. The Havasupai Native Americans occupy a reservation in a remote area of the Grand Canyon west of the national park.

Supai, the only village on the reservation, located in Havasu Canyon on Havasu Creek, is accessible only by foot, horseback or helicopter. Depending on one's fitness level and speed, it takes three to six hours to hike to the village from the trail that starts near Seligman, Arizona.

In four hours, we hiked eight spectacular miles from Hualapai Hilltop to the bottom of the canyon. We traveled among deer, ram and fox, past bursts of flowers and trees, and over creeks while we occasionally enjoyed prickly pears plucked straight from the cactus.

Though I was hiking solo I was not alone. My fellow trekkers from our group of 10 solo travelers were always within a half mile of me. This gave me a sense of safety but also the physical and psychic room to experience the grandeur of my surroundings as *though I were alone*.

❧

If you are feeling constrained by a group that you belong to, ask yourself,
"How can I participate in this community and still be who I am?"

LENS

I have learned to live each day as it comes,
and not to borrow trouble by dreading tomorrow.

Dorothy Dix

 In Serengeti National Park in Tanzania, a gorgeous leopard draped itself across a tree branch about 15 feet from our jeep. I should have been grateful just to see it. With another week of safari left to go, this sighting was the last of the "Big Five" animals most sought after by visitors to Africa: cape buffalo, elephant, lion, rhinoceros, and leopard. Instead, I agonized over my inability to take a clear photo of the leopard's profiled face, the coloring of which blended flawlessly with the branch it rested on.

I waited and held my breath with the back of my 35mm camera pressed against my nose, my left hand cradling the weight of the telephoto lens, and the index finger of my right hand poised above the shutter release button. The leopard never turned its face toward the jeep. As I watched through the narrowness of the camera lens, it stood up on the branch it had reclined on a moment before, and crept into a thicket of leaves, taking with it my opportunity for a perfect picture.

As I lowered the Canon AE-1 from my face, I felt cheated. Not only had I missed my shot but I'd also missed the experience of appreciating this magnificent animal in its natural surroundings. I was so focused on a souvenir for the future that I was left empty-handed in the moment. This out-of-body-experience felt familiar, a prickly reminder of missed joys in my persistent attempts to harness tomorrows.

I saw three more leopards before leaving Africa, elusive though they are. As many as a dozen jeeps roared to each sighting, awash in a frenzy of clacking cameras. And, each time, I left my Canon on the seat.

You can miss an experience by obsessing over how to contain it.

THRILL SEEKER

Your time is limited so don't waste it living someone else's life.

Steve Jobs

On the Grand Canyon's South Kaibab Trail, our group had taken its lunch break on two spectacular mesas: Cedar Point and Skeleton Point. Even along the widest canyon trails, two cannot walk abreast comfortably without one person flirting with the cliff's edge. But the mesas offered room to breathe.

Still, I never saw it coming. At Skeleton Point I slipped and fell. As I ambled toward the lookout, sandwiched between two hikers from my group, my feet gave way in front of me and I slammed down on my butt. The front hiker heard the thud that the hiker behind me witnessed. They both came to my aid. I hadn't a scratch, but the memory of the fall would shadow me the full distance of the cliff-exposed Hermit Trail the next day when these same hikers raced each other downhill. One of them told me that she used vacations like these to take physical risks.

I had different plans for my vacation. I wanted to take my time and experience the canyon's splendor. I also wanted to stay alive. I was fearful of the downhills, especially on the dry, dusty gravel that had sent me skidding on Skelton Point the day before. Besides worrying about dying, I was concerned about injury. I had been training for the New York City Marathon, which was less than a month away, and I intended to run healthy and strong.

It was a hot Arizona October. The canyon climbs were long and steep. And I dug in steady and surefooted toward the rim, living up to my astrological sign – Capricorn, the mountain goat.

❦

One of the best kinds of thrill is defining, honoring, and achieving our goals.

LIGHT BULB

What do I imagine would happen if I responded to pain with softness and vulnerability instead of self-recriminations about how I am not doing it right?

Geneen Roth

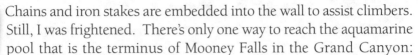 Chains and iron stakes are embedded into the wall to assist climbers. Still, I was frightened. There's only one way to reach the aquamarine pool that is the terminus of Mooney Falls in the Grand Canyon: scale down 196 feet of travertine wall — rock formed by thousands of years of seawater exposure. The wall contains dark, vertical tunnels and over-hanging claw-like formations that look like the set design for the movie *Alien*.

Adding to my trepidation was my guide's gleeful telling of how Mooney Falls got its name: in 1880 Daniel Mooney, a canyon prospector in search of silver, tried to descend the cliffs beside the falls and fell to his death.

Six years before this trip to the Havasupai Indian reservation — home of Mooney Falls — I participated in a ropes course at Boston University's Sargent Center for Outdoor Education in New Hampshire. I was terrified then, too. And I mistakenly believed that forcing myself to endure the terror was its antidote.

Until Mooney Falls, I had spent much of my adult life shaking the proverbial whip at the young, tender parts of myself that would have benefited more from compassion. The roads traveled between New Hampshire and Arizona helped me to take that journey of the heart and leave contempt for my fears behind.

So, I chose not to climb.

In the late afternoon, the Mooney trekkers returned to Supai Lodge breathless with tales of exploration.

"Gina, why didn't you do it?" asked one hiker. "You could have done that, no problem," he said, referring to my fitness level as a marathon runner. I could have, had I been willing to drag the psychological equivalent of a frightened little girl behind me.

Instead, I walked away from Mooney Falls, then turned to my "little girl" and extended my hand.

❦

Life lessons are not journeys traveled in straight lines but are crossroads formed years and miles apart.

HIGHER GROUND

There are so many doors to be opened and I'm not afraid to look behind them.

Elizabeth Taylor

For $89, I spent the day learning to rock climb in Bolton Notch State Park in Tolland, Connecticut. The morning instruction covered safety basics and the afternoon focused on practicing climbs.

Four hours learning how to *belay* – working the safety rope mechanism that tethers each harnessed climber – felt like overkill. Our instructors drilled us: "Never start climbing until the person on belay, the one on the ground holding your line, says 'on belay.' If you're on belay, never take your eyes off the climber and never let go of the rope."

"Start climbing," was all my instructor said at the start of the afternoon as she held my line. I thought, *That's it? We spend half a day playing with rope and no detailed instruction on how to climb?* I stared up at the dark, smooth mass in front of me. Then I turned to my instructor and asked, "How?"

"Put your right foot there," she said pointing to a sliver of a ledge that had appeared flat when I first looked. "And that," she said gesturing above my head to a slight bulge, "looks like a great hand hold."

As I moved up the rock, while impersonating a giant suction cup, new life infused it with language I was beginning to understand. With my breath on its surface, I could discern a structure textured with protuberances of varied scale. Nodes for hoisting my body upward were in large supply though scanty in composition. I now appreciated the morning's focus on safety.

I learned to climb that afternoon by contemplating the rock: *If I pull myself up with my left hand on that knot, I'll need a place to anchor my right foot.* During previous climbing experiences such as cliff-exposed hikes and ropes courses, I had either blocked out my fear or bulldozed through it. Rock climbing, by contrast, presented me with a healthier option: gentle intention.

With rock climbing, I couldn't check out of my body because I had to be connected to it to climb. It was one of the most present-moment experiences I've ever had, hovering several feet above the soil while feeling completely grounded.

What do you resist examining up close?
How can you ground yourself so you feel safe enough to try?

EVOLUTION

The question isn't who is going to let me; it's who is going to stop me.
Ayn Rand

Jan, a 70-year-old author and researcher writes, "I started traveling solo when I was nine when my parents put me on a bus in Hartford, Connecticut, bound for Hyannis, Massachusetts. I was to visit my grandparents, and I can still remember the overwhelming excitement I felt in anticipation of a great adventure. And, today, many years later, I still get caught up in the same feelings, whether I am heading out on a summer sojourn, a weekend in New England, or a Connecticut day trip.

"Fast forward to the mid '70s. I had not traveled alone overnight since I was married almost 20 years before. By now, I was a 40-something wife and mother, working and going to school part time. And, I was weary. I needed to get away and, for the first time, I did not consider asking a relative or friend to come with me.

"My husband disapproved. The concept of a woman taking off by herself was foreign to him, and to me for that matter. How could he understand why I didn't want company? I hardly understood it myself. And, I surprised myself, too, when I answered one of his questions with, 'I don't know where I'm going, but I'll call you when I get there.'

"This was not like me at all. I was a methodical planner, regimented, disciplined, and totally unspontaneous. But there was a force within me, a need to find answers to questions I had not gotten around to asking myself. I waved good-bye on Friday afternoon and headed east towards the seashore."

❧

What would happen if you gave yourself permission to do something you've never done before? There's only one way to find out.

CAREFREE

No trumpets sound when the important decisions of our life are made.
Destiny is made known silently.

Agnes De Mille

Jan continues the story of her solo weekend while in her 40s and married with children.

"When I arrived in Newport, Rhode Island, the Cliff House had just received a room cancellation and I took it. While it was being readied, I ordered breakfast on the patio and basked in the sunshine and ocean air.

"I still remember everything about the room: a window seat that looked out at the sea, the noticeable slant of the wood floor, the odors from the nearby kitchen and the drifting music from the band playing in the lounge below that kept my senses engaged until well after midnight.

"I loved it.

"I spent the afternoon at Block Island, a place I had never visited. Everything seemed magical: the boat trip over and back, the seafood lunch at an outdoor beachside restaurant, browsing in the shops and the wonderful sense of discovery. I bought one souvenir to remind me of Block Island and this weekend: a small balancing toy – a fisherman with a fish dangling at the end of his long line.

"For 30 years, it has stood at the top of my bookcase and I have carefully packed and unpacked my little fisherman with each move. How symbolic he is, reminding me of a time when I was desperately trying to balance my busy life with a need to find myself among everyone I was taking care of personally and professionally.

"The next morning, I walked around the pier area and shopped before driving home, feeling lighter and more carefree than I had in a long time. I had enjoyed an entire weekend, pleasing only myself. When I returned home, I was ready to pick up my busy life where I had left it. And, there was more of me to give."

❧

Take time for yourself. If you feel guilty eating lunch away from your desk or lingering in a bath, let the deprogramming begin.

WHY NOT?

If I were to join a circle of any kind, it would be one that required its
members to try something new at least once a month. The new thing could
be inconsequential: steak for breakfast, frog hunting, walking on stilts...
anything not ordinarily done.

Jessamyn West

 Jan writes, "My first major solo trip came about when a friend told me she was traveling to England. I thought, 'I wish I could spend time in England,' as if there were some magic to it. Later, I asked myself, 'If you want to go to England, why don't you?' There were only two negative answers, but each seemed insurmountable: 'I can't take that much time off from work' and 'It would cost too much money.' But, I couldn't get the thought out of my mind, so I began asking 'Why not?' and 'What if?'

"I remembered reading an article about house swapping, which would save on the major expense of lodging. As for the time off, I told myself, 'You'll never know if you don't ask.' My employer's answer was 'yes.'

"Even though the longest solo trip I had previously taken was only for one week, I didn't give much thought to spending two months in a strange country by myself. Instinctively, I knew that on many levels, this would be a journey of discovery.

"I loved the months of planning and research. Everything fell into place: one month was devoted to two house swaps in different areas of England, while two weeks in London were divided between sifting through dusty genealogy records and exploring this great city. The last two weeks were spent traveling to some of the towns where my ancestors lived and other parts of England I had longed to visit.

"Although it has been 16 years since that trip, the mental process it took to get me there and the lessons learned are still vivid. I've become more adept at hearing and paying attention to my inner voice. When I hear myself saying 'I can't,' I remember to replace it with 'Why not?'"

❧

We can talk about it, dream about it and dissect the fine print.
In the end, only action satisfies our longing.

BLESSINGS

It is solitude that encourages and permits the experience of depth.
Julia Cameron

Jan writes, "One of my sisters had suffered a stroke in Florida where she was living and was in a comatose state. Another sister called to say she was flying out to see her and asked if I would go, too. At first, I refused. I couldn't bear to see my lovely sister in that condition and would be content to remember her during more vibrant times. But, after thinking about it, I decided that the sister who wanted to take the trip might feel more comfortable with someone to lean on. I called her back to say I had changed my mind. I would go after all.

"I was not prepared for her response. She had changed *her* mind and no longer felt the need to go. What a turnaround. By now I was mentally committed so I went to Florida alone. From the moment I arrived, I knew that I was supposed to be there, that some larger force had made it happen.

"During the two days I visited the hospital, I read *Jonathan Livingston Seagull* to my sister, one of her favorite books. Reading this poignant story gave me great peace and I think it gave my free-spirited sister peace as well. And, I got to say good-bye, which for me, was the greatest blessing."

❧

If companionship is a mandate for all of our experiences,
then we will miss out on many of life's blessings.

THE GATES

I think I can make it now the pain is gone/all of the bad feelings have disappeared/here is that rainbow I've been praying for/it's gonna be a bright, bright sunshiny day.

Johnny Nash (from I Can See Clearly Now)

In 2005, I traveled back and forth to New York City from Connecticut to manage my father's estate. On one trip, I noticed bus placards that read, "The Gates." The mysterious orange sketches drew me in. I planned to visit the Web site to learn more. But I forgot; consuming my time and energy were my job, executrix duties and grief over my father's death five months earlier.

No matter. Everyone was talking about The Gates – a public art installation in Central Park. When I realized I would be in Manhattan during its last week – to begin the sale of Dad's apartment – I decided that The Gates was not to be missed. I invited friends to join me but they had plans. So, I visited Central Park alone.

It was a rainy February day. As I approached the park entrance at 64th Street and Fifth Avenue, the aroma of zoo animals and a street vendor's roasted chestnuts were the first triggers of long-forgotten memories.

When I was little, Dad and I went to Central Park like church, where we watched the George Delacorte Musical Clock twirl to chiming nursery rhymes, visited the zoo, rode the carousel and ice-skated at the rink. I remembered my father's joy when watching the monkeys, and how transfixed he was by the quiet intensity of the elephants. Dad was rarely light. But at the zoo, he became a wide-eyed kid.

The first set of Gates was near Wollman Rink. As I stood at the iron railing to watch the skaters, I was eight years old again, my mittened hand wrapped inside Daddy's gloved palm as we skated round and round.

When I was 15, Dad's divorce from my mother changed everything. For decades, he and I struggled to connect. At the rink I began to sob, saddened that the last time he and I had spoken was four months before he died.

Then Dad's favorite song boomed through the rink's sound system: *I Can See Clearly Now.* As it played, I cried harder. I hadn't come to The Gates alone after all. Dad had invited me to meet him at the park one last time – to help me remember the days when all we knew how to do was love each other.

❧

Forgive someone today. Especially if that someone is you.

ADVENTURE

A woman who is willing to be herself and pursue her own potential runs not so much the risk of loneliness as the challenge of exposure to more interesting men – and people in general.

Lorraine Hansberry

 When I tell people that I've traveled to Nepal, they ask me with a straight face if I climbed Mount Everest. And I think, *You've got to be kidding.* I prefer adventures of a different kind.

When I resigned a corporate job to travel around the world, I used it as an opportunity to pursue another goal: to write full time. I had never wholly committed my energies to my lifelong dream of professional writing as I had my corporate career. I was overdue for giving it my best shot.

For three years, I scrambled to earn a living in ways I had never known before, even with part-time work to supplement my freelance income. The challenge of those years included massive personal downsizing, moving three times to trim housing expenses and often choosing between eating well and paying rent.

During this period, a close friend was divesting herself of portions of her estate for tax purposes. I was one of several recipients of a five-figure gift. I used part of it to take a break from my starving artist existence and travel to Nepal for three weeks.

Nepal was in the midst of a Maoist guerilla uprising. Though many of my friends thought I should reconsider the trip, my existence at home felt so tenuous and unpredictable that political unrest in Asia barely registered.

In the end, three weeks of hiking in the foothills of the Nepalese Himalayas was child's play compared to my life back home. I trekked through friendly villages on trails that overlooked luminously green rice terraces, sipped Sherpa tea, sat around a campfire and watched a local shaman infuse a villager with spiritual medicine for his aching shoulder, and tested my cardiovascular system at an elevation of 6,500 feet. When I returned home I was ready, once again, to face life on the edge.

∞

Each of us has our definition of adventure: ending an unsatisfying relationship, returning to school, parachute jumping or training for a marathon. Go ahead. Get your thrill on.

RISK

Avoiding danger is no safer in the long run than outright exposure.
The fearful are caught as often as the bold.

Helen Keller

 In the weeks before my departure for the Himalayas, I received several e-mails from friends: "Have you read about the trouble in Nepal?" Yes, I have. "Are you still going?" Yes, I am. It would not be my first vacation in a region turned newsworthy because of violence.

Now I could add Nepal to my list of risky vacation spots; three weeks after Maoist guerillas broke a four-month truce with the government, the king declared a state of emergency.

The State Department advised against traveling to Nepal. Yet, when I compared the locations of the troubled territories concentrated in the east and west, to the largely central towns and cities listed on my itinerary, I did not find a single match.

Next, I followed every Nepal news story for two weeks leading up to my departure and learned that the terrorist group – estimated at 5,000 in a country of 24 million people – was not targeting tourists.

Finally, I booked my trip with an experienced, reputable company with little to gain by willfully placing its customers in harm's way. I interpreted receipt of my air tickets as a green light.

Was I at risk by traveling to Nepal? Yes. Was it inordinate? I concluded no more so than if I had visited an American city experiencing a wave of drug-related killings. Was it worth it? Absolutely. And not only because I lived to tell about it.

My travel decisions are among my many moment-by-moment opportunities to responsibly exercise my risk muscle and protect it from atrophy caused by imagined fears.

❧

Risk: no full life occurs without it.

TRUST

*It's hard for women to wish for something. It's like they think they'll jinx it.
That's a big mistake. You have to pay attention to your dreams.*

Michele Huneven

 I wanted to mail a couple dozen thank-you cards before spending three weeks in Nepal. I didn't have time to write them before I left home, so composing notes filled the hours of the early legs of my plane trip.

When I arrived at Los Angeles International Airport, I was proud of myself for connecting with friends and extended family before leaving the country for almost a month. But then an airport employee told me, "No mailboxes." They had been removed for security reasons. My trip came three months after September 11, 2001.

Though I appreciated the increased security measures, I felt frustrated. A National Guardsman suggested I take a cab to the post office. I declined because I didn't want to risk missing my flight. Everywhere I went I kept getting "no" as the answer to my mailbox question, yet I felt a persistent nudge to keep asking.

When I queued for my connecting flight to Bangkok, a customer service representative who was directing flow to the gates confirmed mine. His open energy and pleasant face encouraged me to ask once more about mailboxes at LAX.

"There are no mailboxes anywhere in the airport," he confirmed. "But if you'd like, I'll mail your cards right after I leave the terminal. I promised another passenger I'd mail this," he said, pulling an envelope from the pocket of his suit jacket. I hesitated. I had hoped that an airport employee would offer to mail my cards. Now that my wish had come true, I questioned it.

"Do you trust me?" he asked, reading my face and smiling. "If not, you can hand the cards to your airline counter representative."

"You promise?" I asked, as I handed him three hours worth of note writing.

"I promise."

⬥

*To believe that we can have what we want is an act of
trust – not only of others but also, ourselves.*

WISH

It takes as much energy to wish as it does to plan.

Eleanor Roosevelt

Frances writes about her most memorable solo travel experience. "When I was 66, I was planning a trip to Honolulu to visit my uncle when the thought came to me that Honolulu was half way to Australia, and Australia was on my wish list, so why not fulfill that wish? So, after three days in Honolulu, I flew to Sydney where I stayed for 17 days.

"I had no preconceived idea of what Sydney would look like. It happens to be beautiful, with glass skyscrapers surrounding a harbor. Everything fans out from the harbor and when you look across it you see the Opera House. I used the ferries – a primary mode of transportation – and buses with the same ease as I use the subways in New York City. Because Sydney is small, I walked everywhere, too. By the end of my first week, I was a confident citizen with an American accent.

"The Opera House was a grand highlight for me. I attended a gala event by the Sydney Symphony and went back to the Opera House on a different occasion to see "Scenes from a Separation" by the Sydney Theatre Company. I took a bus tour to wine country, and Featherdale – a wildlife preserve – and up into the Blue Mountains. It was coming on to summer in Australia and I went to Bondi Beach and took a day trip to Manley Beach via ferry, where I sat by the ocean, had lunch overlooking the water and walked through the town before heading back to Sydney."

Don't wait for a genie to grant your wishes. That power is yours.

PRACTICE

If you want the rainbow, you've got to put up with the rain.
Dolly Parton

When I traveled to Nepal it had been more than a year since my last solo trip. Before that, I had explored the Andes with a friend. Though I've experienced almost 30 years of solo moments on the road, I was nervous to fly to Asia alone (even though I had been there before), wondering too, if I had what it took to trek the foothills of the Himalayas. *The Himalayas.* Though I would not be any higher than 6,500 feet in elevation, the reputation and mythology of this mountain range filled me with anxiety. I was not in the best physical condition at that time in my life. It seemed like more adventure than I could handle.

The last time I had flown to Asia from the United States was when I moved to Singapore almost 10 years earlier. The idea of flying 30 hours to Nepal caused in me an amorphous dread that I couldn't shake until I hit a flight milestone: completing the 11-hour stretch from Los Angeles to Tokyo.

Now Nepal was real. Surviving the transpacific flight with minimal discomfort and misadventure helped me to rediscover my travel legs. My body and psyche remembered: we have done this before and we can do it again.

❧

Practice makes comfort. Expand your experiences regularly
so every stretch won't feel like your first.

LUXURIATE

There are no short cuts to any place worth going.
Beverly Sills

 "That's a long flight," observed several friends about my plane ride from the United States to Nepal. This was not my first trip to Asia, so I knew that total flying time would be about 30 hours. Given the dry, economy-cramped environment of airplanes, dwelling on the length of the flight was counterproductive. Instead, on the longest leg from Los Angeles to Tokyo, I treated myself to three consecutive mind-candy movies and a cover-to-cover read of four back issues of a favorite magazine.

Under what other conditions could I have indulged myself for 11 uninterrupted hours? Maybe if I spent an entire day in bed and unplugged the phone – an unlikely scenario.

Originally, I considered not packing the magazines in my carry-on, rationalizing that they were too heavy. Why drag them on the plane when I could read them comfortably at home? But the reality of being months behind in my magazine reading convinced me that if I hadn't made it a priority before my trip, I likely would not do so afterward.

When I wasn't reading or watching movies, I drifted in and out of sleep, in sweet surrender to my natural rhythms.

❦

Indulgence comes in all varieties: a mouthful of gourmet chocolate,
a hot stone massage, a week in Paris or 20 uninterrupted minutes to get
lost in a book.

INFORMED DECISIONS

Risk is at the heart of all education.

Willi Unsoeld

In early December 1992, religious riots between the Hindu and Muslim communities in northern India gave me pause before visiting the country later that month. I was living in Singapore and the riots were major news throughout Asia. *The Straits Times*, Singapore's largest newspaper, covered it daily.

I consulted with Singaporean colleagues, some of whom had just returned from visiting family in India. They told me, as did the newspaper reports, that the violence was contained to certain geographic locations far from where I would be traveling in the northern states of Uttar Pradesh and Rajasthan. Though there had been nationwide response to the riots, it largely took the form of peaceful demonstrations.

India was a country I longed to experience. Because I was living in Singapore, I was only five hours away by plane. Not visiting India would have been like canceling a trip to Chicago because of violence in Philadelphia. I had nearly a month to read the news reports, further query colleagues and consult my intuition. All the evidence said, "Go."

❦

Follow your heart. Then root its longing with the facts.

BAD DAYS

If you are never scared, embarrassed, or hurt,
it means you never take chances.

Julia Soul

 On the second night of two solo weeks in India, I wanted to run back to Indira Gandhi Airport.

Having read about the notorious logistical challenges that tourists encounter with India's rail service, I arranged for car transport between cities to save time and hassle. But the Delhi travel agency through which I had booked my trip did not follow my instructions. On my second night, my guide escorted me to the Delhi rail station – instead of a private car – where, at midnight, I boarded the overnight mail train to Bikaner, a desert town 283 miles north.

As the only woman and foreigner in a fully-occupied four-berth compartment, I learned firsthand what my guidebook described as the "True India: If not 50 percent of the fun, 90 percent of the experience." To spend the night in a sleeping compartment with three strange men was unthinkable. It would be like walking into a hotel room in the United States to find three men sprawled on my queen size bed.

My standoffish guide was no help as he had disappeared to wherever he planned to lay his head for the ride. In our hovel of a compartment, my three roomies began to disrobe – shoes, socks and slacks – then change into nightshirts. I sat on my top bunk attempting to rub the disbelief from my eyes. The men didn't seem to be paying me much attention. Still, I wondered if they'd try to rape or rob me as I slept. I decided not to stick around to find out.

I searched for a train official to help me change compartments. But my bulbous duffel, the train's narrow aisle, and the crushing rush of passengers rendered my efforts futile. Exhausted and worried that I might lose the one bed with my name on it, I squeezed my way back to the compartment.

Once inside, I padlocked my duffel to the bunk as my guidebook recommended. I invoked the Universe's protection and silently gave thanks that I had learned on previous trips to wear a flat money belt against my skin vs. a protruding fanny pack. Then, I closed my eyes and whispered, "Welcome to India."

❧

Bad days happen. Meet yourself emotionally
wherever you are on any given day, whether that day is spent at the
Taj Mahal, in the Serengeti or in your living room.

MY CHOICE

The greatest part of our happiness depends on our dispositions,
not our circumstances.

Martha Washington

 Penny, a 48-year-old customer service director, took a solo business trip to Orange County, California, from Utah where she was living at the time.

"I had to go there to do some training," Penny writes. "I didn't know anyone, not even the people I was training. The sessions lasted all day, and in the evening, everyone went on with their own lives. I sat in my hotel room with a Coke and a bag of Doritos. I hated it. But it was one of my first solo trips so I didn't handle it well. Now I venture out more.

"What I like about solo travel is the opportunity to meet new people. At the same time, I don't have to follow an agenda to accommodate someone else. I can stay in the hotel or go out. It's my choice."

❦

Often, we act as though we are being forced to live our lives against
our will. Let this be a reminder that we can choose.

FUN

Freedom is just chaos, with better lighting.

Alan Dean Foster

 Penny, who regularly travels solo for business, decided one day to travel solo for pleasure.

"I needed to get away and have some fun so I flew to Las Vegas. I went there because I could get lost in the crowds. I enjoyed it and I felt totally comfortable being there by myself even in a restaurant, which is unusual.

"I stayed at the Luxor Hotel. In Las Vegas, you can walk up and down the street and stop into any casino for a river of fun. I rode the roller coaster on top of New York New York, went to the M&M store and bought every color they had, bought a cool lamp in the Luxor shop, saw Blue Man Group...it was awesome. And not once was I uncomfortable. People there are too busy having fun to pay attention to you!

"However, I love people. I like sharing my time with others so I wouldn't want to travel solo all the time. But I will definitely do it again."

❧

It's official. You only need a party of one to have a good time.

RHYTHMS

Rhythm is our universal mother tongue. It's the language of the soul.
Gabrielle Roth

Fifteen years ago, when the last of my watches broke, I didn't replace it. I realized then that I had allowed clocks to govern my behavior. I no longer wished to be driven by external time. I wanted to manage my time from within.

I felt at home at Kathmandu's Hotel Vajra in Nepal, where the rooms don't have clocks. Throughout my first night, I awoke periodically after finally crashing from 30 hours of flying. Had I a clock or watch, I would have obsessed over the number of remaining hours until my wake up call. This would have caused the sleep deprivation I was trying to avoid. Instead, I allowed my body its adjusting rhythms – a moonlit tango of wakefulness and sleep.

Without help from me, my rhythms would find their own time, in their own way as they had throughout human existence. Demanding otherwise, through evolutionary arrogance, would have delayed the return to balance that I craved for myself as much as my body did for me.

❦

Each of us knows when it's time to wake, eat and rest.
We don't need to read a clock for these activities; we need to listen.

TREASURED MOMENTS

You never know...that's what makes life interesting.

James Clavell

 From Kathmandu, Nepal, en route to our trek in the foothills of the Himalayas, we stopped in the neighboring city of Patan across the Bagmati River. For the rest of our group of six, Patan was no more than a bathroom stop and a spin past souvenirs. For me, it was an opportunity to interact more deeply with the Tibetan and Nepalese cultures, and to spend time with my guide outside of the dynamics of the group.

Sher, a retired Gurkha soldier, led me to a dark, tiny café with a sod floor. We sat across from each other at a short, wood table the size of a chessboard and enjoyed a smooth cup of Tibetan tea made with local herbs and yak butter. Sher had made this moment a personal goal when he learned earlier in the trip that I drink tea, not coffee.

We were on a short break so there was not much time for extended conversation but the gesture was dear and the memories distinct: the gleeful woman who served the tea; steam rising from the white porcelain cups with no handle; a woven table cloth; squat chairs.

When I recall my visit to Nepal, what comes to mind is my first view of Mount Everest during my flight from Bangkok to Kathmandu. I also remember the sun's morning light on *Macchapucchre*, one of the famous peaks of the Annapurna range, nicknamed "Fishtail" for its shape. Though my Tibetan tea break lasted no more than 10 minutes, it stands among these memories as a highlight of my trip.

⊗∾

The treasured vistas of our solo journeys are not always about the landscape.

RIGHT NOW

Life is uncharted territory. It reveals its story one moment at a time.
Leo Buscaglia

 After enjoying a New Year's Eve dinner at Nepal's Dwarika's Hotel in Kathmandu, I was about to turn in at my lodge when I received a call. "Madam, please join us for dancing and drinks," said an official-sounding voice of a lodge staffer.

It was 90 minutes until the New Year. When I entered the dining room, a fire blazed, perfuming the room with toasty wood. Glittering streamers festooned the ceilings and columns, and professional Nepalese musicians and dancers performed on an intimate corner stage. The drinks and fresh popcorn were free.

To my left sat a vocal, merry group, the only female member of which smiled and beckoned me over to their table. "Are you alone?" asked Sabina, a German expatriate who was the lodge manager.

"Yes, I am."

"We can't have that on New Year's Eve," she said. "Come join us."

I had become quite content with my solo celebration in the Himalayas. And though the beginning of my evening never hinted at it, I was delighted to later share company with a cadre of international travelers.

The countdown began, and at its conclusion Sabina and I toasted with imported champagne. We hugged to the sound of horns and popping balloons. "Happy New Year!" Sabina yelled. Then she paused, eyed me quizzically and asked, "What is your name again?" We broke into hysterics as I shouted my name through the din of music and merriment. I don't think she heard me. And I didn't care.

⬯

We can't script every detail of our lives. But we can solve the riddle of fulfillment when we plan ahead while simultaneously embracing the surprises of each moment.

DIRECTIONS

We are not born with maps, we have to make them.
                                        M. Scott Peck

 In Nepal, I was one of two solo travelers in a group of six that included two couples. On a free afternoon from our tour activities, we ventured on foot from our hotel into Kathmandu's Thamel district. I had planned to take off on my own. However, one of the wives insisted that I stay with the group, and assured me that my company was welcome.

I get turned around easily, and Thamel was busy. Surrounded by new sights, sounds and aromas, it would take little distraction for me to lose my way. So, as the husbands walked ahead and their wives followed while engrossed in conversation, I tracked our route in my travel journal.

The men – retired military officers – turned multiple times as they followed their noses within the labyrinthine district. After a couple of hours, the night sky crept overhead. So, I decided to head back to the hotel. The couples were free to do as they chose. However, they decided to walk back, too.

This time, I led the way. When I took the first turn – at a giant blue and red "SNOWPAL TREKS AND EXPEDITIONS" sign – one of the husbands said, "Gina, that's the wrong way." I said, "No, it's not." I had chosen that landmark precisely for its garishness and size. I held out my notebook and said, "While you were shopping, I was taking notes. Our hotel is this way." And I started walking.

The couples followed. Silently. After a mile, the terrain began to look familiar to all of us. In the end, they thanked me, though it wasn't necessary.

Taking care of myself was.

❧

No matter how many people love us or vow to take care of us,
in the end, we are responsible for ourselves.

MAPS

Life's challenges are not supposed to paralyze you;
they're supposed to help you discover who you are.

Bernice Johnson Reagon

I was excited about temporarily relocating from Maryland to northern California to troubleshoot a contract for my employer, until I learned the details of my new assignment: drive hundreds of miles each day to rural areas to conduct employee meetings. Five days a week. For four months. As a Manhattan native and lifelong subway rider, I had obtained my driver's license only two years earlier.

I drove in circles almost daily, relying on information from locals whose hearts were in the right place, though their directions often were not. With gritted teeth, I turned to maps.

The men in my life had been the map readers, beginning with my father when he drove my mother and me from Manhattan to Virginia during summer vacations. He didn't trust my mother to read a map. Exasperated, my father would pull over, examine the map himself, and chastise my mother for her lack of skill. I witnessed these scenes as a child from the back seat of our rental car, engulfed in silence for miles afterward. I've feared reading maps ever since.

But I would not jeopardize my career. It was time to learn. That California spring I discovered how to trace a map's spindly red and black tributaries leading to my destinations. It was the season when my sense of direction and self trust began to emerge over the course of 8,000 miles, flowering into a confidence my mother could not summon in my father's presence, and rooting in me a conviction that I would always find my way.

❧

Travel in the direction of what you resist. On the way, you will meet a
version of yourself who has been seeking you.

WANDERER

I never panic when I get lost, I just change where it is I want to go.
Rita Rudner

 When Mary, a 50-year-old life coach, was 42, she traveled solo to Oaxaca, Mexico, to join a workshop called "Sacred Heart, Sacred Places" sponsored by The New England Art Therapy Institute.

"On a day when we had free time," Mary writes, "I walked to the *zócalo*, the equivalent of a town square in New England. It was about a two-mile walk and I can still remember the different scenes that passed by me like a movie.

"As I sat eating lunch, I heard the angry cries of women's voices. When I looked up, marching before me was the parade for the International Day of the Woman. Women and children held huge banners painted with women's veiled faces and deeply sad eyes.

"On my way back, I got lost. I don't speak Spanish but managed to communicate with a man who was working in a garage who pointed me in the right direction.

"When I returned from the *zócalo*, it was dark and my feet were blistered. But I felt elated that I had ventured out on my own. I had a deep knowing all day that I would be okay.

"On that walk, I learned that I could do anything I put my mind to. I don't have to know every detail of how I will accomplish my goals. I don't even have to know the way or speak the language. Help is there when I need it."

❦

Distinguish between getting lost and losing your way.
The first is a shift in direction. The second is the absence of perspective.
Cultivate perspective and you will be able to steer home.

INDEPENDENCE

Only those who risk going too far can possibly find out how far they can go.

T.S. Eliot

Jeanne, a 65-year-old hospital chaplain writes, "Believe it or not, the first time I remember traveling solo was when I was 48. I decided to drive to Philadelphia to see my daughter at college during parents' weekend.

"I felt excited and liberated about taking this trip by myself, and also somewhat afraid that I would get lost, encounter car trouble, or look foolish if either happened. However, like a good little former Girl Scout, I was prepared.

"So as not to become lost, I sent for my TripTik, guidebooks and maps from AAA. So as not to be stranded, I bought a cell phone and renewed my AAA road service. So as not to be governed by fear of being thought foolish, I remembered my connectedness to every single traveler on the road and every person I would meet on the journey. As I set out, I began to pray for each driver I passed.

"I felt pleased with myself and proud of my courage and accomplishment when I greeted my daughter at Bryn Mawr for her special weekend. Having been very dependent on a husband for almost 30 years of marriage, I felt as if I were growing up and learning how to make my own way in the world."

∽✖✑

When you declare your independence,
the person from whom you are setting yourself free is you.

COURAGE

*All of us make a pilgrimage whenever we set ourselves
outward bound for inner voyaging.*

Julia Cameron

Jeanne recalls the route she took during her first solo car trip to Philadelphia.

"I decided to travel from Connecticut straight through to New York and over the George Washington Bridge, mostly because I was scared of going that way. I was familiar with the Tappan Zee Bridge and would have much preferred that route, but I knew that the only way to get past fear is to go through it. As it happened, I did take a wrong turn and found myself in an unsavory neighborhood near the GWB, but I also found that I could get out of there and back on track.

"It was a life-changing experience to learn on this trip that if I make a mistake, I will find the wisdom and the courage to get through it by following my inner guide.

"For example, I was wedded to the idea of moving to Nebraska to serve as a chaplain but when the opportunity fell through, I discovered that taking the job would have been a mistake. Also, I bought my first car by myself. It wasn't the best car for me but it was the one I thought I could afford. I hired a mechanic to inspect the car, and the sale hinged on his approval. When he advised me that the car had been in a collision, that gave me a second chance to buy the car I really needed.

"This new way of looking at mistakes has been extremely liberating and has allowed me to take many more risks."

❦

*Mistakes help to sharpen your next steps.
They don't prove that you shouldn't try again.*

TRAINS

One must never look for happiness: one meets it by the way.
Isabelle Eberhardt

 The Tranz Rail is a privately owned consortium that operates New Zealand's railways. The train seats face each other across a table, restaurant style, so no passenger is staring at the back of another's head.

I had looked forward to the quiet, solace and scenery of a three-hour, 230-kilometer ride on the Tranz Alpine, one of the railway's most scenic routes through the spectacular Southern Alps – the longest and highest mountain range in New Zealand.

I ambled through the train aisle then sat opposite two little girls who seemed more interested in each other than in me. Or, so I thought.

"Twins," they informed me by way of introduction, minutes later. Eleven years old. Yes, they knew they looked nothing alike. The younger one explained that even though she looked older she was born 12 minutes later. They were from Dunedin. Yes, I'd been there. Yes, I am American. They were en route to join their mother and father who had relocated for their mother's new job. Mom was a real estate investor who bought and managed rest homes where the girls lived with their family.

I laughed out loud at the twins' stories of their nursing home antics, including wheelchair races down the halls. I asked questions about their country, and we admired the view during breaks from jointly completing the Tranz Rail's geographic puzzle book for children. Ninety minutes sped by and the twins disembarked.

As the train edged out of the station, the girls and a woman about my age waved to me from the platform through the picture windows. I waved back. Then I settled into my seat to reclaim the quiet I had initially sought, only to realize that I was sorry to see the twins go.

❧

Avoid the temptation to force a moment so you won't miss the one with your name on it.

PLANES

Granted that I must die, how shall I live?
Michael Novak

 Two hours into a smooth flight from Texas to Oregon, our jet encountered some of the worst turbulence I have experienced in 30 years of flying. The plane was full and I was traveling solo, trying to appear nonchalant. I checked the demeanor of my fellow passengers and noticed that no one else seemed disturbed by the severe jolting and rocking.

Between moments of calm, the plane pitched and dropped sharply in altitude. No longer able to maintain my composure, I put down my book and gripped both armrests. A woman sitting across the aisle and one row back, who appeared to be well into her 80s, caught my eye and yelled, "Don't worry, honey; the first 100 years are the hardest!"

I burst into laughter even as the plane continued to dip and swerve, completely disengaged from the fear that had seized me moments before. I leaned forward, turned toward the woman and mouthed, "Thank you."

The turbulence continued for another 20 minutes but I remained calm, replaying the woman's comment in my mind. I recognized, for the first time, that traveling solo is one thing; dying solo is a completely different matter.

If the plane were going to crash, all the white-knuckling in the world would not stop it. Faced with such an immediate inevitability, I knew I could make peace with it. What had frightened me, though, was the thought of doing so without any final human connection. The woman on the plane had given me that. I knew that if it came to it, she was the one I would turn to, smile and mouth, "Good-bye."

⚬⚬⚬

Never underestimate the lingering effects of a dash of spontaneous comfort.

FAITH

One learns by doing a thing; for though you think you know it,
you have no certainty until you try.

Sophocles

Pedestrian advice from my guide, Hang, for managing Saigon's traffic: "Walk out slowly, don't step back." By walking out slowly, I gave drivers the fullest opportunity to maneuver around me. It was crucial that I not move quickly or change direction by stepping back or else a driver might not react in time and cause an accident.

My Manhattan upbringing had conditioned me to look for an opening and then bolt when crossing a busy street. Hang shook her head, wagged a tiny index finger in my face and repeated, "Walk out slowly, don't step back."

Hang and I exchanged good-byes at the airport in Saigon and I departed Vietnam's largest city for Hanoi, its capital. There, I stayed at a hotel in the French Quarter, walking distance from the must-see Water Puppet Theater.

When I left the theater at 10 p.m., cars and motorbikes packed the main street without pause in traffic flow. There were no light signals either on this busy strip in a city of three million people. As I monitored the unyielding wall of vehicles, I realized Hang was right.

I breathed deeply, laid down more than three decades of experience, and put my trust in a 97-pound woman whom I had met only days before. Then, as if propelled by some otherworldly force, my right foot stepped out into the street followed by my left. My eyes fixed straight ahead on the curb opposite me as I whispered to myself, "Walk out slowly, don't step back; walk out slowly, don't step back..."

Trust what feels true even if that truth requires you to
ignore what you know.

COMMUNITY

*There is no exercise better for the heart than reaching
down and lifting people up.*

John Andrew Holmes

 As I walked through Seattle's SeaTac airport, my rain stick caused quite a stir. Every comment from "Nice stick!" to "What's that?" followed me to the gate waiting area.

I had been in Seattle on business and took in a few sights, among them Port Townsend, a New-Age tourist town in the Olympic Peninsula. At one of the many shops on the main strip, I spent an hour examining the large rain stick inventory before settling on the size I wanted for the price. My new rain stick was four feet long, four inches in diameter and had a sound that echoed the soothing showers I'd heard in the jungles of Costa Rica, Malaysia and Thailand.

Some travelers recognized the rain stick for what it was – a percussive instrument used by Chilean natives in the belief that it could bring about rainstorms. The travelers commented on its heft, style and weathered beauty. More people, though, had never heard of a rain stick. I was delighted to introduce them to it.

Every few yards, I offered inquisitive adults an impromptu concert. It was a joy to watch their eyes shine and the muscles in their faces soften. They asked me where they could buy their own rain stick and then thanked me for the respite.

When I reached my gate, children gathered around me and asked to play it. Men and women buried in their newspapers or the airport television paused to listen and offer a smile.

On board, the flight attendants stored my rain stick in a special place because it was too large for an overhead compartment.

When I landed in Connecticut, it was raining.

❧

*When we establish human connections within the context of shared
experience we create community wherever we go.*

PURPOSE

*All of us want to do well. But if we do not do good, too,
then doing well will never be enough.*

Anna Quindlen

Allison, a 37-year-old horticulturist, vacationed solo for the first
time at age 35.

"I read an article about ways to use your vacation to help others through
volunteerism. Global Volunteers was one group the article mentioned. I
visited their Web site and looked into their projects. Many were overseas, and
they also had some here in the U.S. in places such as Wyoming, Montana, New
Mexico and Arizona. These appealed to me because I've always wanted to go
out west.

"They had a project open in Arizona that wasn't too expensive because
it included room and board. Volunteers were responsible for their round-
trip travel, spending money and a registration fee. Some expenses were tax
deductible. The project was working with children, teaching community
classes and distributing food and school supplies. I decided to just go for it.

"I joined my 'team' in Tucson not knowing anyone. I wound up meeting
a great group of women and created new friendships through our common
experiences."

❧

*The help we give to others creates the ripple of
good feeling we give to ourselves.*

DREAM

We all have possibilities we don't know about.
We can do things we don't even dream we can do.

Dale Carnegie

 In 1989, my boss announced that he was taking a six-month leave of absence from work to travel the globe. Stunned, I thought, *How does a person do this*? Peter had saved $20,000. He'd purchased a "Round the World" airplane ticket that would take him to 21 countries in six months. He would backpack between cities and stay at hostels and low-budget hotels.

I was aware that people took off to discover the globe but until Peter's announcement, I hadn't known any of them. I thought such adventures were reserved for international jet setters and Manhattan socialites.

As we walked along the waterfront of Baltimore's Inner Harbor, Peter's tales of anticipated adventure became white noise. I didn't hear another word he said because his news had opened the rabbit hole and I had climbed in: if Peter could travel around the world, so could I.

During the next several years, I took globetrotting courses, read how-to books and researched transportation options. My travel file grew as I discovered that there are as many ways to see the world as people in it. But the idea of traipsing around the globe on my own put me on overload. I couldn't imagine negotiating trains, planes and automobiles by myself, and bouncing between hotels.

Seven years after my boss' announcement in Baltimore, I received a cruise brochure advertising a world tour. The itinerary was limited but the brochure raised an option I had not considered, one that felt more manageable and less vulnerable, especially if I wound up traveling on my own. I added the brochure to my file knowing that one day, a cruise line would offer an itinerary with my name on it.

❧

Yes, you can.

THE LIST

Make a list of 25 things you want to do before you die.
Put it in your wallet and refer to it often.

H. Jackson Brown, Jr.

In 1999, on a January day in Connecticut, I sat next to a young truck driver who towed my car to the garage for a new battery. He asked me if I was single, then, why I wasn't married. I said it wasn't on the list. "What list?" he asked. I told him about the list in my wallet, inspired by a quote I read in a women's clothing catalog; "make a list of 25 things you want to do before you die. Put it in your wallet and refer to it often." Intrigued, he asked me what was on it. "Travel around the world," I said. At the time that phrase crossed my lips I had no clue that I was six months away from making good on that 10-year dream.

Given the previous reactions of others – deafening silence or a flippant, "Wouldn't we all?" – I didn't expect much of a response. The driver surprised me though, when, after a few eye blinks, he asked, "Who would you go with?"

During my late 20s, when I first dreamed of going around the world, I had hoped to share the experience with a companion, not from any romantic notion but because I was afraid to go alone. Many of my friends loved the idea of traveling around the world but were not prepared to act on it. Yet for me, the call to go was so strong, to ignore it would have guaranteed a life of emotional torment: I imagined myself an old woman, lamenting how I had not followed my dream, and how that decision, in turn, had created a blueprint for a timid, shrunken life. The potency of that vision overshadowed the fears that had been holding me back. I knew that whenever I took my world trip, it would be solo.

So, on a wintry day in Connecticut, I answered the tow truck driver's question, "Who would you go with?" using one of my father's favorite expressions: "Me, myself and I."

❧

Sometimes our dreams are affirmed in the most unlikely ways by the most unlikely people. That's why we need to speak our commitment out loud.

CROSSROADS

The little things? The little moments? They aren't little.
Jon Kabat-Zinn

 While in England in 1998, I bumped into a woman I had met on a Mediterranean cruise a year earlier. On both occasions, we had traveled with the same local college in Connecticut, where we live.

We ran into each other at Kennedy Airport on the return from London, and while discussing other travels I told her about visiting Egypt earlier that year. She wanted to learn more about my trip because she was booked on an Egypt tour in a few months. This conversation sparked a get-together back home in Connecticut – we discovered we live six miles apart.

From my new acquaintance, I learned about the travel company through which she had scheduled her Egypt tour. Without my knowledge, she put my name on the company's mailing list. I began to receive its brochures, which highlighted spectacular itineraries at reasonable prices.

One year later, I received a brochure that advertised a four-month world cruise. The exotic itinerary boasted stops in ports such as Papua New Guinea, Morocco and Easter Island, none of which I had visited.

At last – the world cruise with my name on it.

After two sleepless nights trying to figure out how I would rearrange my life to travel for four consecutive months, I made the down payment on the trip of my dreams. This decision caused a domino effect of resigning my full-time job to take the trip, launching a freelance journalism career by writing about my trip for a newspaper, and planting the seed for this book.

All because a woman I barely knew put my name on a mailing list.

Life only plants the seeds. It's up to us to help them grow.

PRIORITIES

*Regret for the things we did can be tempered by time;
it is regret for the things we did not do that is inconsolable.*

Sydney J. Harris

 Two weeks before I set sail on a four-month cruise around the world, I found a lump in my left breast. I told the Universe I had heard its previous calling to live life more fully. Wasn't walking away from a full-time job to globetrot for nearly half a year sufficient proof? I didn't need a cancer diagnosis to underscore the message.

Within 48 hours of my primary doctor's examination I had a mammogram, ultrasound, an assessment by a nationally renowned oncologist and a decision to make. If I had cancer, would I postpone my trip and stay home to treat it, possibly spending my last months alive battling disease? Or would I spend my final days on earth fulfilling a dream?

During the 24-hour wait for the diagnosis, I decided that no matter what, I would have my trip around the world because if I didn't go then, I might never go. Fortunately, the lump was benign. My x-rays were clear and, like never before, so were my priorities.

❧

Tomorrow is promised to no one. Prioritize today accordingly.

TESTED

The difference between school and life? In school, you're taught a lesson and then given a test. In life, you're given a test that teaches you a lesson.
Tom Bodett

In April 2000, I boarded the MV Riviera, a 300-passenger cruise ship, in Cadiz, Spain, to begin my dream trip around the world. The ship was scheduled to sail for four months. On day 40, the cruise line declared bankruptcy when the ship was in the middle of the South Pacific Ocean, shortly after we'd set sail from Easter Island, Chile. All passengers were forced to disembark in Tahiti the next morning.

Whenever I tell the story of my bankrupt cruise, this is the part where everyone bursts into laughter and says, "Stranded in Tahiti. What a hardship!" Unfortunately, there was nothing funny about my having resigned a full-time job to travel for four months only to learn that one month in, my $13,000 trip was over.

Also, I was writing a paid, weekly column about my travels called *Journey with Gina* for *The Hartford Courant* – Connecticut's largest newspaper. I'd pitched the online column to the paper as a way to jumpstart another long-held dream: to become a professional writer. Four months of bylines in a two-time, Pulitzer prize-winning newspaper was a great platform for launching that career. But if the trip ended, so would my column. I would return home, out of work and burdened by the grief of unfulfilled dreams.

It was nighttime when the news of bankruptcy rolled across the ship like a wave. The passengers' anxiety level was palpable. Some people were in denial, refusing to prepare for disembarkation. They told those of us who, like me, expressed concern over refunds, that we lacked a sense of adventure and the ability to go with the flow.

Though I'd made acquaintances on the ship who knew my story, the significant sacrifices I had undertaken to be on that cruise were inexplicable to these relative strangers. I couldn't get anyone to understand that my life had just blown up.

So, I purchased an overpriced bottle of cream sherry at the bar and swigged half of it as I sobbed. Fully crocked, I returned to my cabin and packed.

The study book for life's tests is the whole of our experience. Though we may feel unprepared, tests appear only when we are truly ready to ace them.

STARTING OVER

Vitality shows not in the ability to persist but in the ability to start over.
                                                                    F. Scott Fitzgerald

Tahitian authorities seized the world cruise ship I was on for non-payment of fuel bills dating back two years. When we arrived in the port of Papeete, passengers formed lines as long as the boat to retrieve passports and obtain logistical updates from the purser. Fortunately, I was one of 60 passengers out of 300 who'd purchased the cruise through a legitimate travel agency that had flown representatives from Australia to meet us. They whisked us off to the Sheraton Hotel. And, within 24 hours, I learned that I would obtain a full refund.

As we waited for the final arrangements for flights back to the U.S., the travel agency treated us to gourmet dinners and magnificent day tours to neighboring islands. I could enjoy none of it; I was anxious about the uncertainty of my situation and preoccupied with options for a plan B. I didn't want to go home, and with a full refund on its way, I didn't have to. But what now? I needed a plan, and I needed it fast: within 36 hours my travel agency plane ticket to the U.S. would expire.

Before I left the U.S. I engaged the services of an independent travel agent who booked day trips from some of the ports on the ship's itinerary – a canopy adventure in Panama, a trek in the Andean mountains and a Kenyan safari.

When I learned the cruise was ending prematurely, while still at sea, I had e-mailed Joan and asked her to suggest options for a new world tour. Several faxes, countless e-mails and two days later, Joan had a plan: travel in New Zealand for two weeks. This would give her time to arrange my new itinerary including airfare and hotels. English speaking and only a five-hour plane ride from Tahiti, New Zealand was an ideal location to reestablish my footing and calm my nerves while working with Joan to keep my travel dream alive.

When I settled in at my Auckland hotel, I caught up on my latest e-mails from readers who had been following my trip on the newspaper's Web site. Many were of the "You go, girl!" variety from women cheering me on for my pluck and perseverance. One e-mail, though, had a different tone. It was from a new acquaintance who opened her message with, "Sounds like you could use a friend." I stared at the hotel computer screen and let the tears stream down my cheeks.

❦

When life events mimic shattered glass, carefully locate the pieces then gently pick them up.

LETTING GO

A journey is like a marriage.
The certain way to be wrong is to think you can control it.

John Steinbeck

 I visited the port city of Funchal, Portugal, on a cruise ship scheduled to travel around the world. My mission: purchase a vintage bottle of Madeira. At the farmer's market, a merchant's display of colorful woven handbags beckoned me inside the shop, which also contained the best collection of vintage wines in the market for the right price – 4400 escudos or $22 for my 15-year-old bottle.

One month and six ports later, my cruise ended prematurely in the South Pacific. But I began my new world tour in French Polynesia before heading to New Zealand. My first adventure on the new itinerary: hop a freighter to Bora Bora from Tahiti.

From the time I learned about the freighter, I had 90 minutes to get to the dock before it left port. To prepare for it, I spent an hour on the floor of my hotel room triaging the sprawl of contents from a large suitcase filled with months' worth of belongings. What to take? What to ship home? What to leave behind?

During five of those frantic 60 minutes, I debated lugging that bottle of Madeira. Other than two weeks in New Zealand, I had not yet received my itinerary from Joan, my travel agent in Connecticut. I didn't know if I'd be in one place long enough to enjoy the wine. Hauling it once uncorked seemed absurd. And, what if the bottle broke? I hadn't come prepared to protect glass; I thought I would be on a cruise ship.

So, I let it go.

Leaving my cherished Madeira on the hotel bed marked the beginning of my new journey, one in which I would continue to release possessions, attitudes and beliefs – an act that would lighten my load and propel me forward around the globe.

Much of what we acquire in life isn't worth dragging to the next leg of our journey. Travel light. You will be better equipped to travel far.

NEW ME

The important thing is this:
to be able at any moment to sacrifice what you are for what you could become.
Charles Du Bos

 I've always wanted to visit Bora Bora, French Polynesia. When I found myself in Tahiti after my cruise went bankrupt, I learned that Bora Bora was a 20-minute plane ride away. But it cost $250 – too pricey given my limited freelance writing income and the month-long wait for my cruise refund.

I learned about an overnight freighter to Bora Bora for $50, one way. The price was perfect but a *freighter*? Even in my 20s, I never embraced roughing it.

Aching to take advantage of the unexpected opportunity to visit Bora Bora but looking for an excuse to skip the no-frills freighter, I grilled the Sheraton concierge about what to expect. She confirmed that the freighter's accommodations were austere, but "You must go," she purred in a fluty French accent. "Eet weel be ahn ahdventurrrre."

Six weeks on a cruise ship and four days at the Sheraton in Tahiti left me ill-prepared for the dock scene that awaited me at Vaeanu. The freighter was a stubby pug of a vessel with crackling green paint and overhead cranes. If there were any tourists among the teeming populace of passengers, they disguised themselves well.

All eyes were on me as I dragged a large duffel, knapsack and a computer bag up the wooden ramp one at a time, globules of sweat flinging from my body. No cabin steward or hotel bellman stepped forward to lend a hand. Instead, a surly woman in a brown muumuu splayed with oversized white flowers, commanded me in French to pay the extra luggage fine.

The next morning I awoke in Taha'a, one of the four leeward Society Islands and the last stop before Bora Bora. From Taha'a the freighter set sail again in the cool morning air, under a bright, clear sky. A short while later, I pointed to the cloud-shrouded peaks of the magnificent green landmass I had seen at a distance during the new morning. Cloaked in the esteem of my transformation from tourist to traveler. I asked a passing crewmember, "Bora Bora?"

"Oui. Arrive."

❧

Few experiences are more satisfying than becoming
someone we always imagined we could be.

UNEXPECTED PLEASURES

Out of clutter, find simplicity.

Albert Einstein

 By the time I reached French Polynesia on my world tour, I had visited seven countries and spent 40 tumultuous days and nights on a doomed ship. I had earned a rest.

On a 10-minute Air Tahiti flight from Bora Bora, I arrived on the island of Huahine, a lush jungle Shangri-La untouched by mass tourism. In four leisurely hours, I circled Huahine on a rented scooter. There's plenty to see – the vanilla plantation, the archaeological sites at Maeva, the black pearl farm, and many small, isolated beaches. But I'd grown weary of the sightseeing putt-putt of stop, look, go and stop again. Instead, I wanted a more fluid, visceral experience: wind-yielding green, white and turquoise breakers, sun and speed.

With the thrust of the accelerator and the curve of each bend, the landscape turned more diverse and remarkable. Nothing resembled what had gone before it. Warm and cool all at once, the open road was the only place I had to be, on a bike on an island for a day.

❧

At times, productivity means doing nothing at all.

CALLINGS

Follow your bliss.

Joseph Campbell

 At 33 years old, Barbara left a job to become self-employed and needed a break in between.

"I went solo to Mexico for a photography and Spanish class at Instituto Allende," Barbara writes. "I flew to Mexico City and then rode three hours on a bus into the mountains of San Miguel de Allende.

"What I like most about solo travel is that you can bounce wherever you want. Maybe you made plans to turn left at the next street but when you get there, turning right looks more interesting – like in the book, *The Tattooed Map*, about the woman who travels with a male friend. She travels to write. He travels to find aesthetic treasures for his clients because he is a decorator.

"They set out to Morocco, which she loves. After a couple of days and unusual encounters with a local man, she develops a tattoo on her arm that grows mysteriously. It turns out to be a map and she follows it..."

❦

When a thing beckons you to explore it without telling you why or how, this is not a red herring; it's a map.

LET'S GO

The soul of a journey is liberty, perfect liberty, to think,
feel, do just as one pleases.

William Hazlitt

 When Carol turned 40 years old, she traveled solo to Alaska for a 19-day vacation.

"I flew to Anchorage and spent a couple of days before the start of a bike trip," Carol writes. "The trip was with a tour group but for most of my time on the road I was by myself. We took the train to Fairbanks, rode our bikes down Richardson Highway to Valdez, took the ferry to Whittier and rode back to Anchorage. We covered approximately 400 miles that week.

"I then left the group and spent the next week at Kennicott Glacier Lodge. I hired guides and went ice climbing, white water rafting and took a bush plane to the top of a mountain for a day hike. Then I spent more days hiking, reading and writing. Afterward, I meandered back to Anchorage, stopping and staying in little out-of-the-way places for about five days. Some would say that everything is out of the way in Alaska!"

How far are you willing to go to create the life you want?

CONNECTIONS

There is something about the unexpected that moves us. As if the whole of existence is paid for in some way, except for that one moment, which is free.

Rose Tremain

 In April 2000, I embarked on a four-month world cruise. Nearly two months later, the cruise ship was seized in Tahiti for questionable financial practices by the owner. Fortunately, I received a full refund. Still, I was in French Polynesia without a clue.

Though New Zealand was not included in my original itinerary, it was now within commuting distance. The tiny, two-island commonwealth had never interested me because of its distance from the United States – an unfathomable plane ride. But I needed to settle at a destination less costly than Tahiti to plan my next move.

In the capital city of Wellington, I stumbled upon *Te Papa*, New Zealand's national museum, where I discovered the exhibit, "Journey of the Heart: The Travels of Frances Hodgkins." Born in 1869, Frances left her home in Dunedin, New Zealand, at age 31 to study painting for a year. Except for a brief visit after her mother's death, for the remaining 47 years of her life, she never returned to New Zealand. In a letter home, Frances wrote, "...perhaps I ought to have been content with what was a very interesting life but I felt I was only groping; that I had not realized myself..."

For me, Frances became another role model for how to explore the edges of a nontraditional life.

I was 16 years old when the epiphany that I would never marry or have children flashed upon me like a comet in the night sky. Its remnants settled as a deep truth, the understanding of which lovingly promised to reveal itself to me over the course of my life. I was almost 40 years old before I moved from judging that path to embracing it with fuller expression. Frances gave me permission to do that. Had my cruise not gone belly up, she and I likely never would have met.

❧

Relinquish the notion of lost opportunity and try on a new reality:
"Where I am is where I'm supposed to be."

NEVER GIVE UP

Only she who attempts the absurd can achieve the impossible.
Robin Morgan

 I arrived in New Zealand at the start of winter. Mary, an attendant on the Tranz Rail train, tried to purchase my Ecuadorian sweater right off of my back. She asked me what I had paid for it and then offered me money. I told her that I was traveling for five months, my sweater was the only outerwear I had with me and I would not relinquish it during New Zealand's winter. Besides, I love my sweater.

She would not back down. This charming, good-humored woman continued to increase her offer as though bidding at an auction. Then, as if I hadn't said a word, Mary gave me the New Zealand dollar equivalent of two and a half times the cost of the sweater in U.S. currency: $75. She made me promise to buy one for her when I returned to the U.S. five months later.

I reluctantly took the money and offered no guarantees. The sweater had been a spontaneous purchase at a weekly Manhattan street fair years earlier, and I lived 110 miles away. I'd have no idea if the merchants would still be around.

Initially, I thought Mary had given me extra money as incentive to follow through on her request until I added it up after my shopping expedition to New York: $23 for the round trip train ride from Connecticut to Manhattan, $30 to buy the sweater and $22 to ship it to New Zealand. Exactly $75.

This was an intercontinental transaction governed by larger forces to be sure.

If you don't ask, you don't get. But if you ask and don't get, ask again.

INVITATIONS

Trust in yourself.
Your perceptions are often more accurate than you are willing to believe.
Claudia Black

 A chatty British woman sitting behind me on the InterCity Coachlines bus from Greymouth to Queenstown, New Zealand, introduced herself. Her travel companion sat across the aisle from me but didn't speak. When we discovered we were staying at the same hotel, the chatty traveler invited me to dinner.

Shortly after checking in, the woman knocked on my door and for 20 minutes trashed her companion who turned out not to be what she had expected in a travel mate. I had an early instinct that these travelers and I did not share values but the woman's betrayal of her companion clinched it. I no longer wanted to share a meal with this duo. And the more I thought about it, the more I realized I never had.

From the moment I boarded the bus at Greymouth, I fantasized about a quiet evening with myself: a favorite meal, a long bath and – especially because I don't own a television – an HBO movie. Yet I accepted the dinner invitation anyway.

In five consecutive months of travel I can count on one hand the number of truly miserable evenings I spent. That was one of them. From then on, I vowed to make more authentic choices about the people I spent time with, even for the duration of a train ride.

Stand up for yourself by not standing yourself up.

CHOOSE WELL

It is better to travel alone than with a bad companion.

Senegalese proverb

 Carol, a public relations professional, traveled to Jamaica with a friend "who proved to be very hard to get along with as a traveling companion," she writes. "I enjoyed myself the most after I started going off on my own. She wanted to 'hang out' with Rastafarians. I wanted to snorkel.

"On a different trip to Mexico, I had to convince a woman friend that we were not handcuffed together. We were in a church in Chamula in Chiapas, a beautiful, moving place.

"Groups of Indians were gathered around candles on the floor, which was covered with pine needles. One man was crying out to God because he was 'sick in the chest' and afraid he was going to die; bronchitis is a big deal when you don't have antibiotics. I was so touched, I started to cry as I made my way farther in.

"My friend announced, 'I've had enough of the church.' Nothing about it moved her. I said I wanted to go in, up to the altar. Fifteen seconds later: 'I've had enough of the church.' I told her to go outside and have a cigarette since she smoked. It took a long time before I traveled with someone again."

❧

Take your time and ease into commitments.
What you learn during the preview will foreshadow the main event.

CHILL

It's not the load that breaks you down, it's the way you carry it.
Lena Horne

Two New Zealand airlines sent me ping-ponging between their service counters at the Auckland airport in the hour before my flight to Sydney, Australia. Their representatives were searching for an electronic reservation I'd booked two weeks earlier. The poor communications between these two carriers – one listed the flight, the other operated it – led to an "It's-not-our-problem" approach to customer service. I was getting nowhere. And my increasing frustration and anger didn't help.

They were wrong. But that didn't matter. What mattered was that beyond the bureaucracy and computer glitches were humans who had the power to complicate my life. So, I laid down my battle gear.

With the clock ticking toward take-off, my instincts told me to focus on making a human connection with just one of the two agents. Even if the agent believed her airline was right and the other one wrong, I hoped her desire to help a distressed traveler would triumph over the need to blame.

I replaced the righteous, accusatory edge in my voice with a vulnerable tone. I softened my facial expression and breathed my shoulders away from my ears. Then I retold the story of how I purchased my tickets, this time with more detail in the hope it might offer problem-solving clues. Also, I made sure the agent knew I had been on a bankrupted cruise that had dumped me in Tahiti.

Finally, I pleaded. "I understand that you can't guarantee that I'll make this flight, but I've checked out of my hotel and I have no place to stay. I'll be grateful for anything you can do." This was not manipulation. This was the truth.

My new approach caused a Herculean shift in the attitude of the ticketing agent whose fingers flew across her keyboard, so hell bent was she to get me on that plane.

Had anger remained my tactic, the gates to the Sydney flight likely would have remained closed to me. Even if they hadn't, the consuming nature of anger would have had me snorting all the way to Australia. Instead, with minutes to spare, I finally moved through security, boarding pass in hand.

❧

We often mistake letting go for giving up. Knowing the difference between the two can make all the difference in the end.

PASS IT ON

There are more truths in 24 hours of a life than in all the philosophies.

Raoul Vaneigem

 I arrived in Cairns, Australia, during early winter. It was close to 6 p.m. and getting dark when I decided, "It's now or never – I have to go for a run." I had spent most of the day sitting in planes and in hotel shuttle vans; I couldn't stand being sedentary any longer.

I donned my running gear and headed through the hotel lobby to the oceanside walking path. On the way out, I saw Robert, the hotel's shuttle van driver. Earlier, when he'd picked me up at the airport, we discovered that running was a common interest.

"Going for a run?" Robert asked.

"Yes," I said, "but it's pretty dark out."

"It's quite safe," Robert assured me, "I run all the time at night." I explained to Robert that as a man he was less vulnerable than I was. "When women are afraid to be out at night," I said, "it's not because we fear other women." The smile fell from Robert's face. He said, "I know."

I felt reasonably comfortable along the esplanade because it was active with tourists. Still, as a general safety practice, I kept my eyes in the back of my head.

As I ran to restore my energy and shake off the sluggish feel of the day, I envied Robert his gender protection, to run without care for the night. I believed, though, that he had understood what I tried to convey in a passing moment, about how it feels to wear female skin yet live out loud in spite of it, perhaps because of it. And, in his own way and when the time was right, I also believed he would pass that meaning on.

❦

A heavy message is better delivered with a light hand.

LOST AND FOUND

We shall not cease from exploration and the end of all our exploring will be to arrive where we started and know the place for the first time.

T.S. Eliot

 Australia's Great Barrier Reef boasts 2,000 varieties of fish, 400 species of coral and 3,400 individual reefs. During my afternoon at Moore Reef, lifeguards roped off a large section for snorkeling. As I assessed the distance from the pontoon to the back rope, I asked myself a question that had come up several times during my trip: "How much adventure can you stand?" It seemed unlikely that I'd visit Australia again, so I flippered to the farthest buoy.

The coral presented like a dense underwater forest awash in bright greens, flamingo pinks, fiery oranges and gemstone blues. The interior of expansive caves hinted at oceanic life as I floated still. Animated tendrils darted back and forth, pulsating and creeping upward. Transfixed, I swam farther – to the reef's edge.

The Big Blue took me by surprise: no coral or fish. No sense of depth or objects of relativity. Just blue. My peripheral vision was consumed by it. And like the many who tell of near-death experiences, this was a moment of joy, not fear, a desire to move through and not look back.

But there came a tug on my cord, the one that signaled me to turn around. Now I fully appreciated the legend of the siren's song, serenading sailors to their deaths, the beauty of a thing wooing beyond reason and the desire to live.

As I swam toward the pontoon, I felt the ocean's suctioning churn. My alliance now reversed, I fought my way back to the protection of the reef.

✑

When you push beyond self-imposed limits, take care not to lose yourself along the way.

INTIMACY

Tact is the knack of making a point without making an enemy.

Isaac Newton

 During a refueling stop on a flight from Tokyo to Bangkok, I met a woman who was originally from Iran. The woman was headed to Phuket, Thailand, a coastal city with stunning beaches. She had plans to meet friends there for New Year's Eve and, later, travel farther south to the island of Ko Samui.

We were traveling in mid-December. In one breath, I learned that she usually spent the holidays alone, had a pinched nerve in her back and so that's why she chose islands as vacation spots so she could swim vs. hike, which she loved but couldn't do, what with being in all that pain, which precluded her ability to exercise for the last month and now, in the absence of activity-induced endorphins, she was depressed. She had taken a sleeping pill to get her through the remaining seven and a half hour leg to Bangkok and would I wake her up if need be when the plane landed.

I finessed a "no" so polite that I never actually said the word. An entire flight crew was at her disposal, and I also needed to rest. More than that, I felt she was asking too much of me without our having established any connection. We were not seated together – she was one row in front of me – and we had spent no time talking during the first half of the plane ride. Still, I might have been more inclined to respond to her request had she left an opening for reciprocity rather than rush at me with her needs.

As I nestled into my seat and reflected on the encounter, I reminded *myself* to create a window for give and take when meeting other travelers along the way.

❧

Sharing our story is one way we create intimacy. And like a good novel, it's more engaging – and lasting – when we allow it to gradually unfold.

ROLE MODEL

With hair, heels, and attitude, honey, I am through the roof.
RuPaul

On a day tour to the region of Galilee in Israel, I met a Belgian woman whose outfit I admired for its practical yet elegant comfort. I mentioned that I had observed European women travelers the world over who managed to dress similarly. I felt that American travelers could use a few international style tips.

"How do you do it?" I asked.

"First," she said, rattling off a list of to-dos like the mother of the bride on the morning of the wedding, "No colors; only neutrals – tan, navy, khaki, white." Yes, Americans love to sport every color in the rainbow. I gave myself points for wearing olive drab.

"No shorts. Always wear a mid-calf skirt or slacks." By most of the world's cultural standards, we also like to flash the flesh. I, however, was wearing pants. I've always been a modestly dressed traveler.

"Only natural fibers. No synthetics." I noticed her elegant, beige linen vest. I sported a polyester pullover.

"Absolutely no sneakers. That's the biggest tip-off that you're American." I was wearing black leather walking clogs with a rubber sole. Many trips ago, I had learned the no-sneakers strategy for blending in with the international set vs. announcing my nationality with my feet.

"Jewelry: keep it simple. Earrings shouldn't dangle." She tugged at the delicate pearl in one of her lobes. "And, one single-strand necklace. That's it. No rings." I passed the rings and necklace portion of "How To Dress Elegantly European" but I failed earrings. And make-up, like jewelry, must be equally understated.

Finally: nails. She pointed to mine and said, "European women never do that."

"What?"

"Square their nails. That's an American thing." She extended her hand.

"Always, always, a soft oval."

Experience is a master teacher, even when it's not our own.

CROSSING OVER

The truth is there is nothing noble in being superior to somebody else.
The only real nobility is in being superior to your former self.
                                    Whitney Young

 After hiking a half day to the village of the Karen Hill Tribe in northern Thailand, it was time for me to bathe.

The shower was a closed wooden shed with a palette-over-concrete floor. In one corner stood a metal tank filled with water. On top floated an orange plastic scoop. One end of a hose was connected to the tank at its spout; the other end rested in the water.

I sulked, squirmed and produced assorted moans of disapproval while reminiscing about the palatial bath at The Oriental – one of Bangkok's five-star hotels. Finally, I told myself, "Get over it. You're in the jungle for four days." I tried not to imagine how many tourists or villagers had come before me. I kept my rafting sandals on and retrieved from a plastic baggie the tiny bar of soap I had plucked from my room at The Oriental. I was careful not to let it drop because I did not intend to pick it up.

During my jungle treks I had obsessed over giant tropical insects and leeches as I waded chest deep in muddy rivers. In this rustic, communal shower, fatal bacteria captured my imagination. Also, I was unhappy with the cold water despite triple digit heat. *So, Princess, would you rather spend your entire trip lounging in a five-star hotel?* I mustered a mousy, "no." Though most of my travel had been to faraway and exotic destinations, until my jungle shower, it had also been well manicured.

I dipped, soaped, rinsed and then dried myself with a spare T-shirt. I slipped a fresh tank top over my head, wrapped a sarong around my waist and emerged from the dark shed a culturally refreshed soul.

❦

It is not so much the grand dramas of our lives that transform us as it is
the tiny one-acts we produce in between.

TICKET TO RIDE

An adventure is an inconvenience rightly considered.
Gilbert Keith Chesterton

In northern Thailand, I strained my knee at the beginning of what was to be a four-hour trek from the Karen Tribe village of Muang Phem to the Red Lisu village of Phamon. Plan B: my guide arranged for my transport with the local mahout.

Phasador, a three-year-old elephant, took me for a bone-jangling, breath-holding, muscle-tensing ride. When he descended into rivers, I used every muscle group to keep from falling out of the chair on his back. When he climbed mountains, gravity pushed my lower back against a knot in the wood. The front raised rim of the chair dampened the circulation in my legs, which I slapped every so often to awaken. This had the added benefit of keeping at bay every species of insect that had decided to join me for the ride.

Tree branches that ordinarily swung far above my head now posed threats to my eyes and skull. For four hours, my gaze never strayed from in front of me, and my arms motored like wipers without a windshield. Though I hadn't taken a step, by the time we reached the village I was exhausted.

But my physical discomfort had yielded to an awareness of an animal who could crush me with his foot, yet shrieked and reared at the sight of a butterfly; a creature who despite his mass, walked without making a sound; a gift of nature who moved trees with a swat of his trunk yet shrank from horses, frightened by the clopping of their hooves.

It was a ride I wish never to repeat, and a memory I will cherish until my last days.

❦

When actors encounter a mishap during a stage performance,
they transform it for good purpose by employing a technique called,
"use the difficulty."
How can you "use the difficulty" in your life?

SLOW DOWN

He who limps still walks.

Stanislaw Lec

 I fell hard at Don Muang International airport in Bangkok. I was writing about my trip for a newspaper and wanted to e-mail my most recent column before heading to Vietnam. I intended to relax when I arrived in Saigon rather than focus on meeting a deadline. Either the Internet or the café's computers were sluggish so it took some time to upload my column and photos.

When I spotted a clock I panicked; it was only 30 minutes before my flight was scheduled to leave. I maniacally paid my Internet bill and bolted through the café door. In my frenzy, I didn't notice the slight rise at the foot of the doorway. I wasn't prepared to step down and I crashed.

Stunned, I lay sprawled on the airport floor, trying to grasp what had happened. My calf-length skirt was hiked up to my thighs, my computer disc lay several inches in front of me, and the bones in my forearms throbbed. I was grateful that I had instinctively used them to cushion my face and skull.

That should have been enough of a signal to slow down. But now I had lost more time. So, I got up and started running again. This time I ran past my gate, missing the sign that pointed downstairs to the left.

I did board my plane in time, but as a sweaty, frazzled mess – not a first on this trip. My world travel dream was darkening around the edges because I was moving too fast. And I was moving too fast because I was trying to do too much.

❧

Treasure yourself for being, not doing.

SIGNS

Flops are a part of life's menu and I've never been one to miss out on any of the courses.

Rosalind Russell

 I knew it was time to slow down when I kept falling during my trip around the world. In Thailand, I fell repeatedly during my hikes between tribal villages. At Bangkok's international airport I took a nasty spill running out of an Internet café to catch my plane. In China, I skidded down stone steps as I left a jewelry factory, cutting the skin on my forearms and the palms of my hands.

This was not ominous portent from the skies; this was sleep deprivation.

When I wasn't touring, I was writing a weekly, online newspaper column about my trip. Often, it was nearly 2 a.m. before I slept for the night. Then I was up by 6 a.m. to eat breakfast and perform morning rituals. I prefer nine hours of sleep but I was getting four to six hours in the two weeks prior to my falls. Sleep deprivation is a choice. And my series of accidents made it clear that I needed to choose differently for the remainder of my trip.

It was tough. I was a woman living a travel dream that also presented an opportunity to launch a professional writing career. It frustrated me to constantly switch from vacation mode to being a first-time reporter seeking to establish a foothold in the business.

I would have loved, for example, to languidly watch the sun set over the gorge in Petra, Jordan, have a second glass of wine at Florian's café in Venice, Italy, or stay up until dawn anywhere. But my laptop had died several countries ago, which meant I had to write my weekly column longhand then type it on computers at Internet cafés all over the world. These extra work logistics lengthened my days. And rather than cut back on touring, I stole hours from sleep.

Though initially torn between work and play, ultimately, I chose to sleep more, tour less and maintain my writing schedule. I could always see more of the world. But my *Journey with Gina* column was a divinely offered career break to which I intended to give my all.

❧

Rest and repose are as much a part of life's journeys as seeing all we came to see.

THE NUDGE

No more words. Hear only the voice within.

Rumi

Claire, a 49-year-old author, traveled with a group who'd gone to India to help prepare for an ashram dedication ceremony. While in the garden with the group, she felt a "nudge" to leave and listened to that prompting.

"I walked out of the ashram and followed an instinct about where to go and stop," Claire writes. "I did that most days while in the northern town of Rishikesh. Whenever I felt a nudge, I left.

"Sometimes, I'd walk miles into the hills or through neighboring communities. Other times, I'd end up only 1,000 yards from the ashram. All the time, however, I'd be walking near or parallel to the Ganges River. And, whenever I followed that instinct, stopping wherever I felt I needed to, there were always people and experiences encouraging me to see with non-physical eyes.

"Though I had traveled on the plane with others, most of the time I was on my own. It was the first time in a long while I had trusted that much. I realized I was trusting my inner voice, the great mother, who was calling me to her side to teach me."

As you consider your next move, practice this definition of trust: the willingness to take steps while simultaneously waiting for "instructions."

WHAT I WANT

If you always do what interests you,
then at least one person is pleased.

advice to Katharine Hepburn from her mother

Lynn recalls her cross-country train trip from Cincinnati to San Francisco and back.

"It was a blast. I got a sleeper compartment, which was just the right size for me. The advantage was I could write as I sat there, see into the backyards of America, and lie on my bunk and watch the stars for miles and miles across the Great Plains. The only disadvantage was that meals were included with my ticket and the railway served wonderful apple pie à la mode. I ordered it with every entrée and gained seven pounds that I haven't been able to lose since!

"I LOVE traveling on the ground by car and train. It is much more personal than flying. If I were younger, I'd go hiking or biking, which is even more personal.

"I have never taken a trip alone that I hated. Of course, there have been some moments that were difficult, or that I wish I'd handled differently. But the joy of trying new things and being in charge is almost more than I can stand. To eat when I want and pee when I want and see what I want – what a treat!"

At least once a month, indulge that part of you that always knows
what you really want.

DO IT ANYWAY

Right down to the wire/even through the fire.
David Foster (from Through The Fire)

 Lynn writes, "The toughest trip (but still delightful) was going to Europe alone. I went partly to attend a conference in Amsterdam, but afterward, I took the train to Paris, then to Nice, Avignon, through the Alps to Geneva, then Brussels and then home. The hard part was not speaking any language other than English and being too shy to speak up to those around me. I wound up smiling and saying 'merci' a lot.

"I loved the sights, but it was frustrating not to have anyone to exchange words with. Also, I spent too much time getting train tickets and hotel rooms, going to the bank, and finding bathrooms.

"One of the hotels was a genuine fleabag, which I made the mistake of paying for three nights in advance. I didn't have nerve enough to change that. The door was flimsy and didn't lock, so I pushed a dresser against it to sleep. But there were lovely lace curtains in the windows!

"Even with the difficulties, this was an incredibly wonderful trip and I would do it again. Only next time, I'd use a center-and-spoke method of travel. I'd get a hotel in Paris or some other city and go out from it for day trips so I wouldn't have to keep finding new hotels. And I'd study a little more French, too."

Stop now and always wonder. Press forward and tap the wonder.

INTUITION

Intuition is the spiritual faculty that does not explain.
It simply points the way.

Florence Scovel Shinn

As I walked toward the Sun Dong An shopping plaza in Beijing, a young, neatly groomed woman approached me and introduced herself as a university student who enjoyed speaking with visitors to practice her English. She studied art and asked if I'd like to view her work. Before I could respond, a young man appeared, equally polite and articulate. He welcomed me to China.

"Where's the art?" I asked.

"Inside," the man said, gesturing toward the building behind me. "Upstairs."

At that point, more than a few bells rang inside my head. The first was that "upstairs" was too vague a locale for an art showing. The second bell was a clear recollection of the woman. The day before, I had heard this woman having the same conversation with two American tourists as I passed them on the way out of my hotel – the building behind me. Bell number three: my hotel had no public art gallery.

I don't know what that couple was up to. I could venture a few guesses, but I didn't stick around to find out. What matters is that I honored my intuition, that highest quality information source deep inside all of us that serves up the real deal while we're clinging to our spin. Though they were educated and polished, something wasn't right about those two. And I didn't allow the appearance of a situation to talk me out of the truth of it.

❧

When your safety is in question follow your intuition.
It will help you balance along the precipice between vulnerability
and adventure.

INSTINCTS

I feel there are two people inside of me – me and my intuition. If I go against her, she'll screw me every time, and if I follow her, we get along quite nicely.
Kim Basinger

 Claire recalls a solo bus trip from Texas to Mexico.

"I crossed the border to Mexico wearing a tight, almost see-through sweater, with an expensive camera around my neck. I was so involved in the sights and snapping pictures, I hadn't realized that I'd stepped away from the touristy part of town. I was now in a rusty, mud-bricked neighborhood where a group of teenage boys began to follow me. One look around and I realized I didn't have a clue where I was.

"Panic hit at first, but then some inner guidance kicked in telling me to fake it. I pretended to be nonchalant because I felt that if I started to run or appeared afraid, then I'd be chased down. So, I sent out a 'guidance radar' to set me back on the path to safety.

"I didn't know which way that was. But I wandered at a brisk pace, turning down roads where I thought there was a chance someone might hear a cry for help, if it came to that. I continued walking, turned a bend and there was the edge of the touristy area up ahead.

"The boys were close behind me at this time. But I pretended to see someone I knew and yelled 'Mark, there you are!' I put on a smile and jogged into the crowd.

"It was a silly thing to do for an American woman to walk practically naked, with lots of camera gear, into a poor community. I felt like I'd intruded on, and disrespected the people. Also, I had not taken good care of myself.

"But I felt like something was sorting out the ways I should walk. I was grateful for those survival instincts and the angels who came to my rescue."

Imagine how fluid life would be if we each had an advisor who, with our best interest at heart, provided clear, objective and decisive guidance. When we trust our instincts, we do.

SAFETY

Travelers are privileged to do the most improper things.
                                                    Isabella Bird

 I lost sense of time while journaling at a restaurant one night on Huahine, an island in French Polynesia. Only after sunset did I recall the absence of street lamps along the dirt road to my bungalow at Chez Lovina.

When the sun was high, I had ambled around town without a plan, map, or the name of the road for Chez Lovina. As I wended my way back through the dark, deserted streets, I remembered that the front office closed at 4 p.m. during off-season.

I hadn't packed a flashlight. I toyed with the idea of requesting an escort from a local before considering that my marginal French might be misinterpreted. Hyperventilating, I pounded ahead on the tarmac, passing hordes of sailors on shore leave from a French naval ship.

With no visible landmarks to guide me, I followed a hunch and turned left. It felt like the right road but I could see nothing in the pitch blackness to confirm it. Rather than prolong my terror, I sprinted down the dirt road, grateful to remember that my bungalow was the first on the right, and that my porch had a light switch.

Talk about not thinking ahead. Talk about not thinking at all.

Now, whenever I travel, I tote a flashlight and I attune to my surroundings. I tuck the business card from my lodging in my wallet rather than risk forgetting the address. This also helps me ask for directions when I don't speak the language.

❦

Practice safety by being informed, alert,
and aware of your surroundings.

SELF-DEFENSE

Learning is movement from moment to moment.
Krishnamurti

 One night in Australia on Sydney's bustling streets, an unsavory character eyed me as I ambled into a Woolworth's to purchase provisions. Minutes later, a woman approached me and asked for $50. Someone had stolen her purse, she claimed, and she needed money to get home. I shot her my native New Yorker look: *Girlfriend, I'm from the city that invented the street scam. Don't even try it.*

Though not unduly concerned by the attention, I wondered why street people were singling me out in a cosmopolitan city where I blended. Then I remembered my sticker.

Earlier that day, I toured the Olympic Village at Sydney's Homebush Bay where security required all visitors to wear an identification sticker. At the tour's end, I had forgotten to remove it. When I realized the sticker had turned me into a walking billboard that advertised "I AM A TOURIST!" I chuckled and peeled it from my T-shirt. Then I stuck it to my travel journal as a reminder to be more vigilant about my personal safety.

❧

If we use our heads as the first measure of self-defense,
we'll likely never have to use our bodies.

PREPARE

If you can find a path with no obstacles, it probably doesn't lead anywhere.
                                                        Frank A. Clark

Mary writes, "Getting ready for an RV trip always involved a thorough checklist, covering everything that the vehicle, the pets or I might need. I learned to run a check on the RV, from tightening wheel lugs and checking required fluids to tune-up and lube. Even though service people did most of these chores, I double-checked them myself, and knew how to handle them on the road if I needed to.

"In those days, I had a CB radio and knew how to use it. Also, I knew what gas mileage to expect and marked out possible stopping places on a map ahead of time. I even carried first aid supplies, such as Ace bandages and splint materials in case of injury, plus extra antibiotics so I wouldn't have to search for a doctor if I got an earache or sore throat.

"I carried a camping directory with me too, so I knew the phone numbers of each site. And I called home each night so people would know that I arrived OK. This is a must, even if you just call for a moment.

"This next one might sound silly, but it's not: I painted my license plate number in huge lettering on the roof of my vehicle, so a police helicopter could spot me in case of a family or other emergency.

"I made it a point to talk with experienced drivers and abided by their advice: 'Never drive in high winds; don't drive after dark or in heavy rain. Have plenty of food and water aboard so you can stop if you need to for three or four days and enjoy it' (as I have done when the weather turned sour).

"In short, my preparations were as thorough as if I were going to fly a plane, leaving nothing to chance. I know all of this sounds compulsive, but being ready for anything enabled me to turn the ignition and fly free, going wherever looked good!"

❧

Be accountable for your choices and actions.
That's the price of freedom.

TAKE IT EASY

The first problem for all of us, men and women, is not to learn but to unlearn.
Gloria Steinem

During my first visit to the Andean mountain city of Cusco, Peru, I didn't take time to adjust to the altitude – 11,000 feet. It was a long morning. I should have eaten a snack, then rested on my hotel bed before my guided afternoon tour.

Instead, fresh from my flight from the sea level city of Lima, I dashed around Cusco's main square running errands, first to a handful of bookstores to purchase a local map, then to an Internet café to check e-mail. Afterward, I attempted to sprint the hill back to my hotel because I wanted to be on time to meet my guide.

I hadn't run far when a disorienting combination of nausea and dizziness left me crumpled on the cobblestone steps.

After several deep breaths, I stumbled back to the hotel and composed myself before my guide arrived. Now I was famished, which only compounded my symptoms. The early stages of altitude sickness had kicked in, leaving me woozy and with a headache that did not dissipate until my return to sea level two days later.

❧

Rather than resist rest and gravitate toward constant motion,
let's experiment with letting go.

THE BROTHERHOOD

It is one of the most beautiful compensations of this life that no man can sincerely try to help another without helping himself.

Ralph Waldo Emerson

 During five consecutive months of globetrotting, I received help from strangers the world over, including men who wanted nothing more from me than the satisfaction of helping a traveler.

Among them were a teenager in Ubud, Bali, who, in the rain, gave me a lift on the back of his motorbike to an Internet café; a Parisian businessman in Papeete, Tahiti, who drove me to the dock to catch my freighter to Bora Bora; a bellhop in Cairns, Australia, who, after his shift, drove me to the all-night drugstore to buy seasickness medication for my catamaran ride to the Great Barrier Reef the next day; my Spanish guide who arranged a temporary fitness club membership in Costa del Sol; and the manager of a hilltop hotel in Panama who cashed my travelers check in American dollars.

Also, there was the French Polynesian freighter employee who clipped my baggage lock that wouldn't open even with the key. I explained what I needed using my personal patois of sign language and rudimentary French. Clearly understanding my meaning, he returned to my cabin with a pair of industrial pliers.

Thanks, again, guys!

***

People across the earth are aching to serve as your ambassadors in one form or another. Let them.

SAVOR

*As I make my slow pilgrimage through the world, a certain sense of
beautiful mystery seems to gather and grow.*

Arthur Christopher Benson

 I took my sweet time in Petra, Jordan, a UNESCO World Heritage Site. Much of Petra's appeal stems from its spectacular setting deep inside a narrow desert gorge. I ambled inch by glorious inch through the passage that ripped through the rock in a prehistoric earthquake, threading my way between ancient inscriptions and chambers carved in whorls of sandstone.

At the end of the gorge sits the imposing façade of the Treasury, Petra's most famous monument featured in the final sequence of the film *Indiana Jones and the Last Crusade*.

The Treasury is only one of hundreds of tombs, temples and façades in ancient Petra, including the formidable Monastery, worth the 40-minute sun-baked rock climb. I drank it all in at my own pace as I hiked up the rocky trail to the Monastery in sweltering heat, wrapping the sarong I had purchased in St. Lucia around my head.

❦

*Call it walking meditation or a neighborhood stroll; by whatever name
suits you, rediscover the art of meandering.*

ROLL WITH IT

We should be too big to take offense and too noble to give it.
Abraham Lincoln

 At night in Petra, Jordan, women weren't out at all. Because my laptop failed early in my world tour, I had been drafting my *Journey with Gina* columns by hand, then typing them at Internet cafés. So, I had to be out to type and e-mail my column to the paper before I returned to Tel Aviv for a flight to Italy the next morning.

Though my hotel was less than a mile from The Petra Internet Café, I wished not to invite undue attention by walking the streets alone at dark. So I took a $1 cab ride.

At 11 p.m., on the way back to the Petra Palace, I struggled to keep a straight face as I rattled off a string of white lies to the cab driver who engaged me in a conversation nearly identical to the one I'd had on the ride out with a different driver:

"Where are you from?"
"America."
"First time to Jordan?"
"Yes."
"You are most welcome."
"Thank you."
"Traveling alone?"
"No, a group."
"How many nights here?"
"Two."
"Are you married?"
"Yes."
"Where is your husband?"
"Beijing."
"Why do you not stay with him?"
"He's working."
"Do you like your husband?"
"Yes, he's a wonderful man."
"What do you do this night?"
"Work," I said waving my computer disc as I hopped out of the cab.

Then, I busted out laughing as I entered the hotel lobby.

❧

When life becomes a game, we'll fare better if we lighten up and perfect our play.

COMPANION

Learn to enjoy your own company.
You are the one person you can count on for the rest of your life.
Ann Richards

 In the city of Hue, Vietnam, I finally found the vegetarian restaurant my guide had told me was within walking distance from my hotel. I looked forward to a quiet meal of my favorite local foods.

I was traveling off-season so the city was still. The restaurant was empty except for a western traveler playing a game of chess with a Vietnamese man who turned out to be my waiter.

Before my dinner arrived, I scanned the restaurant, taking in its outdoor tropical hominess: picnic tables, colored paper lanterns and flowering plants swinging overhead.

The chess player caught my eye, and in an Australian accent said, "Hi! America, right?" He seemed eager for conversation as he waited for his chess partner to return. I was less eager. I smiled and nodded without a word because my hours had already been stuffed with words.

All day, my guide had pummeled me with incessant chatter. Then, once on my own, a tri-shaw driver who refused to understand that I wanted to walk, not ride, followed me for 20 minutes as I ambled toward the shore of the Perfume River.

By the time I arrived at the restaurant, my spiritual body was agitated. I felt a deep craving for peace, silence and the physical space to integrate the events of my day.

Later, at the river, I sat on a pier and watched the gravel miners and fishermen at work, and the tourist dragon boats glide across the water in a moving postcard – a lyrical memory all my own.

A craving for company can yield the surprising discovery that
the companionship we yearn for is with ourselves.

RENEWAL

To know what you prefer instead of humbly saying amen to what the world tells you to prefer, is to have kept your soul alive.

Robert Louis Stevenson

 It was my last night in Vietnam's central city of Hue. Most other tourists sipped cocktails at their hotels overlooking the Perfume River, or rode mopeds and hired tri-shaws around town. Me? I was in a tailor's silk shop at 11 p.m. ordering a dress.

I had to have an *ao dai* – the national attire of the elegant women of Vietnam – a high-collar, long-sleeve, ankle-length tunic with a tight-bodice that is slit from the waist down and worn over complementary slacks.

I was feeling unattractive, what with alternating two pairs of pants, rotating four tops and my hair crying for its overdue perm. My only pair of "dress" shoes – soft, black walking clogs – was scuffed, dusty and caked with mud. And my nail polish had chipped into tiny views of the world map. I ached for a little glamour.

Miss Lam outlined my measurements, promised to sew through the night and then express mail the purple silk creation to me in Hanoi. We were giddy with fatigue as we studied my itinerary, working through the final logistics of our transaction.

In Hanoi, my last night in Vietnam, I tried on Miss Lam's *ao dai*. It fit perfectly. Who are these incredible women who whip up silk dresses in the middle of the night and before getting started, escort you to your hotel on the backs of their motorbikes?

I checked the full-length mirror, smoothing the purple silk along my waist. With a fresh set of nails, my hair in a twist and a shoeshine from Saigon, I felt like a million bucks.

❧

You don't have to spend a lot of money to feel like a million.
A good night's sleep, a quiet walk by the river or a hug from a favorite person will do the trick.

ASK

I've always relied on the kindness of strangers.
Blanche Dubois (from A Streetcar Named Desire)

 Arriving at Peru's Cusco Airport I scanned the crowd for a blackboard with my name on it. Because the travel agency knew I'd be solo, I stepped to the side hoping that its representative would spot me.

No luck.

As I searched for the agency's telephone number, two men approached me and, in Spanish, asked about my lodging. One part of me thought, *Don't tell these men where you're staying.* Another part said, *You need help.*

I pointed to the agency's phone number on my itinerary. One of the men escorted me to a green pay phone. After a few words of Spanish into the receiver, the man nodded, smiled and handed it to me.

"*¿Habla usted Ingles?*" I asked.

"Yes," came the response.

Using a combination of Spanish and hand gestures, the two men instructed me to wait near the telephone so my ride could easily find me.

"*Muchas gracias,*" I said.

"*De nada, Sẽnora.*"

On my world tour, the kindness of strangers didn't end in Peru. I received help from people around the globe, including a headset-wearing businesswoman outside Rome's train station whose electronic toys helped locate my hotel; a man who helped me find my bearings in Paris' *le métro*; and a hotel manager in Tahiti who let me into his office after hours to send e-mail.

❦

Life provides ample opportunity to test our mettle.
When circumstances call for it, let's give ourselves a break
and ask for help.

CUSTOMS

*Chance is always powerful. Let your hook be always cast;
in the pool where you least expect it there will be a fish.*

Ovid

The Peruvians use cocoa tea for many maladies including altitude sickness. I didn't drink the tea on my first trip to Cusco and paid for it with what Andean natives call *soroche*. When I returned to Peru to visit the Inca ruins of Machu Picchu, I didn't intend to miss a moment of it. This time, I was all about that tea. And, it worked.

When I told a friend I'd be traveling to Peru she said, "Please bring me back two boxes of cocoa tea. I'm skiing in Idaho in the fall and it helps with the altitude. Besides, my children love it."

Cocoa tea is available everywhere in Peru, a standard item at any food market. So, I purchased the tea for my friend. On my way back home, I declared it at the airline check-in counter in Cusco.

"You can't take that into the United States," the airline representative told me. "You'll need to remove it from your luggage before checking it." I reminded her that it was tea, nothing more. But she insisted.

Cocoa tea is not an illegal substance. The transportation of cocoa anywhere in the world is illegal only in its raw form – leaves. In that form, cocoa can be used to make cocaine. The tea, which also contains ingredients other than cocoa leaves, is processed. No amount of drinking it will cause a high. And my guide told me that anyone inclined to smoke it would suffer a headache. Some tourists have tried.

I stepped away from the counter. I turned my back and pretended to remove the tea from my luggage and hand it to my guide. That ruse, plus a busy check-in counter, allowed me to keep the tea right where I intended – in my bag.

***

Cultivate the art of maximizing serendipitous opportunities.

EMBRACE

Nothing is better than the unintended humor of reality.

Steve Allen

 In Bali, Indonesia, I adopted the cultural practice of being indirect or silent rather than risk offense or deliver unsettling news.

Runita, my Balinese guide, hesitated when I asked him if we were stopping for lunch during our four-hour drive from Pemuteran in the western part of the island to Denpasar in the south.   I knew the pause meant that the answer was "no" because he was trying to figure out how to break what he thought I'd receive as bad news. Initially, I found his indirectness to be maddening. But I had already spent a week with Runita and I'd finally caught on. I could see the debate taking place behind his eyes.

I thought, *What a liberating custom! Simply refuse to answer a question that makes you feel uncomfortable.*

Four hours passed. Runita never answered my lunch question. Later, he told me that his favorite female movie star was Demi Moore. Given her extraordinary beauty, I chuckled to myself thinking, *It figures.* When Runita asked me, "What's funny?" instead of tiptoeing around an answer that might offend him, I assumed a blank, yet pleasant expression and said nothing.

∞

When you feel yourself resisting differences, lean into them, instead, and have fun with what happens.

SILENCE

And silence, like a poultice comes to heal the blows of sound.
Oliver Wendell Holmes, Sr.

 In Southeast Asia, I enjoyed Vietnam's five big cities – Saigon in the south, Hue and Danang in the center, Hanoi and Haiphong in the north – but my favorite times came with the silence, surrounded by nature.

"China Beach," as it is called by Americans because of its South China Sea location, no longer hosts soldiers on R&R but offers unblemished cooling for bathers around Danang. South of Saigon, the lush Mekong Delta is now peaceful, a fertile lifeline for fishermen, tourist boatmen and fruit and honey farmers. One farmer hosted me at a tea party among his beehives and orchards of dragon fruit, longon and gooseberries. And a one-night stay on Cat Ba Island was not enough to explore its white sand beaches, dense tropical forest and panoramic vistas.

I hired guides in Vietnam to help me navigate remote locations more efficiently than I could on my own. Though they generally were pleasant, I did not look to them for companionship. But my Hanoi guide seemed to feel obligated to provide a steady stream of observations and queries as if part of his job description included "Talk Her Head Off."

As I struggled with how to draw a boundary and still be polite, I succumbed to his geyser of words. As the days wore on, I felt anxious and irritated. When we boarded a dragon boat bound for Cat Ba Island, I finally made my move.

I told my guide I was a little seasick – which was true – and needed some time alone in the fresh air. Then I walked to the front of the boat and left him inside. In four hours, I never tired of the hypnotic, soft jade waters enveloping the thousands of limestone formations in Halong Bay, a 1,500 kilometer UNESCO World Heritage Site east of Hanoi.

Periodically, I turned around to check in on my guide to find him sleeping, reading or smoking a cigarette at the back of the boat, relaxed and seemingly comfortable in silence, too.

❧

Turn off the radio, TV, DVD, iPod, computer and cell phone.
Then, listen.

BOUNDARIES

Boundaries are to protect life, not to limit pleasures.

Edwin Louis Cole

 At the airport in Papeete, Tahiti, I ran into a family of four who had disembarked the same bankrupted cruise ship as I had. They were waiting for a late night flight to Los Angeles, and I was en route to Auckland, New Zealand. The family was playing card games with a 20-something-year-old trio who, like me, was embarking on an extended world trip.

The mother in the family introduced me to the three young travelers and announced that we were on the same Auckland flight. Maybe we could travel together, she suggested with enthusiasm. I was at least game to have a chat, to learn more about the young trio's itinerary. But their silence, stony faces and downcast eyes sent a clear message: *Not interested.*

I was still reeling from the abrupt end of the cruise. Even though many of the earlier mysteries were solved – I would receive a refund, keep traveling and write my newspaper column – beyond two weeks in New Zealand, my itinerary was still forming in the capable hands of my U.S.-based travel agent. I thought, *I'm in the South Pacific about to fly to a country I've never planned to visit, and two weeks from now, I have no idea where in the world I'll be.*

I should have been excited. This was adventure with a capital A. Instead, I suddenly felt lonely. I wondered, *What if it's like this everywhere I go? What if people don't want to be with me?*

But I respected the line that was drawn. Rather than sit with the group, I wished everyone a safe journey and found a section of the airport to call my own.

How simple life is when the lines are clearly drawn.
The drama begins only when we cross them.

RECEIVE

Our internal horizons stretch with our external ones.

Julia Cameron

Originally from Ukraine, Youri and Gallina were a travel agent couple I met in Rotorua, New Zealand. They lived in Auckland and were on what travel agents call a "fam" or familiarization tour to experience the area before marketing it to tourists.

On our day tour, Youri offered his arm when I stepped off our little van, and cupped my elbow as we walked on slippery rocks at a nature farm. I assumed we'd part company at the close of our day but on the way back to the hotel, the couple mentioned the hot springs for which Rotorua is famous. Did I want to join them for a relaxing dip?

I was still emotionally and physically exhausted from the dramatic shift in the events of my world tour and just wanted to sleep. Also, I was squeamish about the prospect of dipping in public waters. But Youri and Gallina exuded a gentle helpfulness I'd not often experienced in my life, a welcome break from managing my own logistics, especially now that I had to gear up to take on the world in a new way. All I had to do was show up in my bathing suit, carrying a towel. The young Ukrainian couple had researched the particulars.

When we arrived at the springs – a potpourri of creatively landscaped pools, moderately populated by young families and older adults – Youri gave me the tour. Each pool was set to a different temperature. The idea was to start at low heat and work up while alternating dips in cooler pools to prevent overheating. Etiquette dictated that one dipped to the waist or neck, rather than swim or submerge one's head underwater.

As the steaming blue-green waters soothed my lagging spirit, I thought, *I could get into this.* I was grateful to Youri and Gallina for coaxing me out of myself.

I was leaving Rotorua the next day. As I prepared to say good-bye, the young couple kissed me softly on each cheek and asked me what time I wanted to meet them for breakfast.

Breakfast?

After our morning meal, they helped me downstairs with my luggage and waited with me until my bus arrived.

❧

Often, the key to getting what we need is simply to let it in.

CELEBRATE

The reward of a thing well done is to have done it.

Ralph Waldo Emerson

 During my last night in Beijing, I celebrated a milestone. China marked the conclusion of the Asian leg of my world tour. After one week in the Middle East, followed by three weeks in Europe, I would conclude my trip around the world, realizing a 10-year dream.

Because I was traveling solo and writing a weekly newspaper column about my trip, I chose to consume little alcohol, preferring to stay clear-headed.

But it was nearing 10 p.m., I needed only finishing touches on my latest column, and I wouldn't need to rise before 11:00 the next morning. So, in the lobby bar of the Song He Hotel, I decided to indulge in a glass of Amaretto, my favorite nightcap.

After ordering my drink, I noticed pockets of businessmen eyeing me, seemingly more out of curiosity than threat or romantic overture. I paid them no mind. When my drink arrived, I took a full-bodied sip. And, with pen and column in hand, I nestled into an upholstered chair.

❧

**If you can't remember when you last basked in your own glow,
it means you're overdue.**

OPEN ROAD

There are years that ask questions and years that answer.
Zora Neale Hurston

Motor scooters have been my preferred mode of transport in India, Bali, French Polynesia, Vietnam and the Caribbean. It's one of my favorite ways to just *be* with a place – not to see anything in particular, but to experience the rush of images, the veil of wind and the freedom of a meandering mind.

I imagine that it feels like flying.

I traveled to six continents over a period of 20 years before I brought that visceral pleasure back home. Before that, whenever I saw someone riding a motorcycle or scooter, I wished it were me.

Why can't it be me? I wondered. Always a long list of reasons: *I can't afford it; it's too cold for too long in the Northeast; I live in an apartment – where would I keep it so no one will steal it?* When I bought a house with a garage, I ran out of excuses.

I live in Hartford, Connecticut – a quiet city with a population of 122,000. There are stretches of back roads that lead to neighboring suburbs where I ride my red scooter – maximum speed 45 mph – while passing as few as two-dozen cars early on a Saturday morning.

My favorite road is in a town called Rocky Hill. The street is straight and flat enough that I can see far into the distance. My favorite moment comes when I turn onto this strip and see no other vehicles. That's when I pretend I'm on Route 66 and gun it while belting out Steppenwolf's *Born to be Wild*.

***

Today is the day to grab hold of your joy.

HUZZAH!

This book has been a journey in itself. Eight years, to be exact. And, like a literal journey, I've met many people along the way who've left their indelible mark on it and me.

Beth Bruno whose editing and feedback significantly impacted the structure of this book to the good.

Sara Davis who gave me the thumbs up.

Janet Davenport and Elizabeth Gibbs, early midwives for the idea.

Michele Deluco, my Comma Queen.

Jeanne Dursi who gave this book her heart.

Robin Grant-Hall who nailed the book's message long before I did.

Carla Denise Marshall Greenleaf who, for the past 25 years, remains constant and loyal.

Jan Mann who had the patience to talk me through the nuances of every literary challenge as only another writer would.

Sharon Mayock who introduced me to Dana Robinson, my designer, and who lent a sharp design eye to the cover.

Marita McComiskey who provided the key to an early conundrum.

Abbe Miller who read and commented beyond the call of "duty."

Liz Petry for copy editing.

Dana Robinson whose visual talents pulled it all together.

Michael Staufacker who's on board no matter what.

The authors on the National Writers Union book listserv who, with grace, joy and eloquence, shared their solo moments on the road.

Jan, Jeanne, Marita, Frances Cano, Chelsey Lovell and all the women who generously shared their stories.

Nan Boyer who helped me find Chelsey whose 20-year-old voice added an unexpected sweetness to these pages, and a reminder to see the world with fresh eyes. And Jan who led me to Frances.

Abbe, Beth, Carla, Jan, Michael and Sharon, the die-hard manuscript readers.

Abbe, Beth, Carla, Jan, Nan, Robin, Ellen Brenner, Pam Craparotta, Suzette Louro, Eunice Medwinter, Julie Olson-Raymond and Bea Srams for reading and commenting on the final introduction.

Isabelle Zarka for Francophone accuracy.

Chris Morrill of *The Hartford Courant* who, eight years ago, sent me sailing with a laptop and digital camera, giving me the break every fledgling writer needs.

Gary Duchane, formerly of *The Hartford Courant*, for being a gentle, supportive editor who went with the flow and gave me the room to find my voice.

The men around the world who helped me safely find my way.

Beth Lipton who believed I could do anything I set my mind to, and who lives on in this book.

Joan Lee, an angel on whose wings I traveled the globe.

Thank you all.

ABOUT THE AUTHOR

GINA GREENLEE is the author of the *Cheaper Than Therapy* series of illustrated inspirational gift books. She was a columnist for *The Hartford Courant* and has written for *The New York Times Magazine, Essence* and *The St. Petersburg Times.* Gina has been a world traveler since age 14 and has visited six of the seven continents. In 2000, she took a solo trip around the world, fulfilling a long-held dream.

Visit
www.ginagreenlee.com